Culture Shock

by the same author

SUPERMAN
THE NAKED MANAGER
CAN YOU TRUST YOUR BANK? (with Norris Willatt)
THE COMMON MILLIONAIRE
THE EUROPEAN REVENGE (with Norris Willatt)
THE NAKED INVESTOR
THE ONCE AND FUTURE MANAGER
THE BUSINESS OF WINNING
THE BUSINESS OF SUCCESS
THE NAKED MARKET
THE SUPERMANAGERS
THE NEW NAKED MANAGER (revised version of *The Naked Manager*)
THE POCKET MANAGER
THE AGE OF THE COMMON MILLIONAIRE (revised version of *The Common Millionaire*)
THE STATE OF INDUSTRY
THE SUPERMARKETERS
THE BEST OF ROBERT HELLER
THE DECISION-MAKERS
UNIQUE SUCCESS PROPOSITION

Culture Shock

The Office Revolution

Robert Heller

Hodder & Stoughton

LONDON SYDNEY AUCKLAND TORONTO

British Library Cataloguing in Publication Data
Heller, Robert, *1932–*
  Culture shock: the office revolution.
  1. Great Britain. Offices. Automation
  I. Title
  651

  ISBN 0-340-52082 5

First published in Great Britain 1990
Second Impression 1990

Published by Hodder and Stoughton,
a division of Hodder and Stoughton Ltd,
Mill Road, Dunton Green, Sevenoaks, Kent TN13 2YA
Editorial Office: 47 Bedford Square, London WC1B 3DP

Photoset by Butler & Tanner Ltd
Printed in Great Britain by
Butler & Tanner Ltd, Frome and London

CONTENTS

ACKNOWLEDGMENTS

In a world revolving at such dizzying pace as that of the electronic office, any writer needs all the guidance he can get. Fortunately, much brilliant work has been published on every aspect of the revolution now impinging on the office and on management. Some of the most valuable material has appeared in the *Harvard Business Review*. I am very grateful to the authors, and to the *Review* for its permission to quote from and cite the articles listed in the text.

Some of the best reporting on the subject has been published over the past several years by *Business Week*, on whose excellent reports I have been most kindly allowed to draw. I am also grateful to the *Financial Times*, an invaluable source on this as on all other business subjects, the *Guardian, Wall Street Journal* and *Fortune* magazine for permission to quote from articles published by them. McKinsey & Co has kindly given me permission to quote from an important article published in its admirable *Quarterly*. The Satex Group has my thanks for allowing me to quote from the report which it commissioned from the Henley Centre, while I am grateful to Unisys Ltd for permission to quote from a powerful corporate brochure.

Some of the chapters incorporate material originally used for my columns in *Management Today* and my articles in *Business Life,* to whose editors I owe a great deal. Two publications which I myself edit, *Finance* magazine and the management annual published under the auspices of the Institute of Management Consultants, have also been most valuable sources. I am very grateful to Sterling Publishing Group, for the opportunity to educate myself through this work. I also owe special thanks to John Kavanagh, who has organised *Finance*'s information technology coverage from the beginning, and who very kindly read the proofs, offering his usual shrewd and informed advice.

Business Books Ltd has kindly allowed me to quote from Charles Handy's important and already influential *The Age of Unreason*. I am also indebted and grateful to William Collins Sons & Co for permission to use a typically pungent and enlightening quote from *Making It Happen*, by Sir John Harvey-Jones: and to Heinemann Professional Publishing for permission to draw on two brilliant works – *The New*

Realities, in which Peter Drucker draws up the agenda for the next century, and *In the Age of the Smart Machine*, by Shoshana Zuboff, which breaks new ground in the exploration of the impact of electronics on management and men – and women.

I am particularly indebted to Rank Xerox (UK) Ltd for setting me off on this path and for allowing me to make free use of the powerful material which it has compiled. The founding role of the Xerox Corporation, especially through its Palo Alto Research Corporation, in many key aspects of the office revolution is acknowledged by all, including its competitors. David O'Brien, the managing director, and his colleagues at RXL have an unusually clear vision of the future, combined, of course, with detailed experience of the present: both have been invaluable to me.

Among many people who have helped me on and along the way, I must especially thank Michael Aalders, of The Grayling Group, who has been father and nurse to the project: my sister Jacqueline Edelman, who processed much of the manuscript: Anne Leguen de Lacroix and Maria Brooks of Magazines International for their assistance: and Ion Trewin and Jane Osborn of Hodder & Stoughton, who have been their usual immensely supportive selves.

INTRODUCTION

Closing the Great Divide

A great cultural divide has opened and widened at the heart of Western society. It is being closed, and at an accelerating pace. But in the process, people's lives, habits and modes of thought will be changed radically – and the shock of cultural change will be felt throughout the West.

C. P. Snow long ago drew attention to the worrying development of two distinct cultures in educated society – the scientific and the literary. In his own person, Snow bridged the two cultures. Few others did, and even today few others do. But over the past decade another cultural split, or bifurcation, has grown, which will affect a far wider constituency – everybody who works in the office environment.

This is not a prediction, not an exercise in futurology. The future is here. Everything described in these pages exists, either in the marketplace, or in the minds of clever technologists whose ideas are guaranteed to become reality inside a very short timespan. These creators are leaders on one side of the new cultural divide – the people who understand, use, create, and exploit the new technology of information. On the other side are the mass of white-collar workers, from chief executives down to junior secretaries, who are not familiar with most of the advances in Office Systems Technology (to use Rank Xerox's phrase), who hardly employ any of its elements, and who have no clear idea of the impact which OST will have on them (or their successors) and their organisations.

To the first culture, that of the literally "informed", or the datacrats, this book will seem simplistic, parading as revolutionary the concepts and capabilities that they have known about, and employed successfully, for years. To the second, uninformed culture, the book may well seem to parade ideas and electronic functions that are irrelevant to their working lives – developments that may, perhaps, become reality some time in the next century, but which can safely be ignored for now. Call this great majority the conformists, for they cling to the

9

conventional past, to which the paper form, in its billions, can stand as monument.

The clash between these two cultures, between datacrats and conformists, is graphically illustrated by the experience of one sales and marketing executive who had recently moved from the computer industry to a leading British multi-national. In his previous company, the population of computers was one to every 1.3 employees. He was able to contact the corporate database for any purpose from his own home; he could communicate through this computer with anybody in the company – his office and his work had become computer-based.

In his new company, whose level of advanced technology in its own businesses led the world, none of this capacity existed. He told me that the contrast was "like going back to the Stone Age". That is the cultural divide in a nutshell. Technology and history have moved on, leaving the majority of the world behind. The longer that organisations and their members take to catch up, the greater the shock of the new must be.

For some, it could be too late. The phrase "competitive advantage" has, like all management coinages, become debased by overuse. But the undeniable fact, as this book seeks to demonstrate, is that companies at the leading edge of the new technology have already achieved lower costs and increased market power by the automation of "structured" activities – the routine tasks that constitute the operational life of the organisation. These structured advantages are being won by those managements which are also more effective at the "unstructured" work of planning, taking decisions, and making things happen – and it is here that the new technology is now starting to have its impact.

Inevitably, the unstructured leaders will establish a far more significant edge: because their enhanced creative powers will perceive where the next structured advantage can be won, and the next. Their domination won't come suddenly, like a clap of thunder. Like the domination of Japan in many world markets, including finance, it will spread slowly, in some cases without being much noticed. The suddenness will not be that of the historical development, but that of its being realised – by everybody, including those for whom by then it will be too late.

The slow take-up of Office Systems Technology by the world as a whole means that, for the moment, there is still time. But by 1992, a couple of years on from the time of writing, the proportion of networked PCs (the acid test of the revolution) should have doubled to 30%. If the rate of progress *halves*, every appropriate PC will be networked by the end of the century. I speak as a late-comer to these developments: until I saw the future/present in Rank Xerox's offices (described in Chapter 19), grappling with other people's words had left me unsure of exactly what was happening in the evolution – rather, revolution – of the office.

That demonstration, and conversations with David O'Brien, the managing director of Rank Xerox (UK) Ltd, Peter Blackmore, marketing director, and Rob Walker, director of strategic business development, set me off on what proved a fascinating journey into areas which shouldn't have been so surprisingly new to me: because I have written about the computer industry in general, and the PC companies in particular, for many years. But the suppliers themselves have been overtaken by the speed of events: only a short time ago, for instance, there simply wasn't the processing power available in PCs to handle desktop publishing, computer-aided design, presentation graphics, large spreadsheets, software applications development and artificial intelligence programs – not even for a single user.

Today, all this and more is becoming available to people whose workstations are connected via a network. This book aims to bring the revolution that is happening – indeed, that has actually happened – to its readers' notice now, with apologies to those who already know it all, and more. Quite possibly, their own familiarity has contributed to the culture gap, not by breeding contempt for the uninformed, but by concealing how enormous the gap actually is. This is the same syndrome that explains the notorious inefficiency of manuals for computer software and hardware. Those who commission and compile the manuals know how to work the machines and programs, but have no understanding of those who don't.

That is only one explanation of the culture gap. Another is the sheer speed of development. Even experts in the industry are uncertain what will resolve a situation in which, at the time of writing, the hardware is racing ahead of the software. But the numbers are almost frightening. In three stages Intel's microprocessors (at the heart of most personal computers) have risen from 1 to 1.5 mips (millions of instructions per second) to 3 to 6 mips and lately to 15 mips and upwards. By the year 2000 – not far away now – the figure for mips could be exactly the same as the date: 2,000.

The power of PCs has multiplied more than fifty times since IBM entered the market in 1981. In this process, the old distinctions between PCs, work stations, minicomputers and mainframes are becoming hopelessly blurred – desktop PCs can already achieve technical performance that, a decade ago, only the world's largest computers could attain. Now genuine *lap-top* PCs are arriving that, with a time-lag of a year to eighteen months, are recapitulating the progress of the desktop. The technical developments will bring the benefits of "multi-tasking" to the "office worker" wherever the office, or rather the computer, happens to be – multi-tasking meaning that a PC can simultaneously print a document, accept new data over a telephone, and communicate with other users via their PCs or workstations.

As the old walls have tumbled, however, new ones have risen. The multi-tasking, multi-user world is the office revolution. But it's bedevilled with conflicts between operating systems, between rival architectures and over industry standards in almost every sector of electronic office equipment. Faced with phrases and names like Unix, OS/2, Micro Channel Architecture, Extended Industry Standard Architecture, emitter-coupled logic, SQL, the user is understandably confused. Worse still, where different standards are used by different companies (and there are some 400 firms marketing PCs alone) the machines get confused, too – and can't work with each other.

To make confusion worse, the price situation is highly unstable. As I write, you can choose between an "engineering workstation", offering minicomputer performance at a price of $20,000, or a personal computer of comparable powers, purchased via mail order, for a fifth of the price. Then, take image-processing, one of the huge advances waiting for most offices to exploit. Had you wanted to digitalise and store incoming messages, legal documents, hand-filled forms, photos, drawings, etc. in the very recent past, the storage would have cost you £300,000. Now £20,000 will see you well on your way.

The combination of tumbling prices and confusing choice is a good excuse for inaction. Give a bad manager a good excuse, and he'll take it. But the obvious fact is that price/performance ratios have already reached the point where future savings are limited by the law of diminishing returns. Today, right now, the office technology can provide immediate benefits, both quantifiable and subjective, mundane and strategic, that will amply justify the expenditure, will pay off still more handsomely as the system is upgraded, and will remain fully effective and economic over a perfectly reasonable time-span.

If you wait for the industry (or rather industries, for the data processing market has fragmented and is still fragmenting) to sort out differences over standards and to arrive at commodity pricing, you will not only wait for ever (for no man knows what technological surprise is about to burst forth), but you will lose immense benefits in the here and now. Whether it's desktop publishing, filing, internal and external mail, networking, decision support or anything else, the manager is no longer buying pigs in pokes. The ability is there to revamp the entire management system into a more effective mode.

That, of course, is the ultimate hurdle. Few managements are quite that enthusiastic about embracing change. But the change is coming, anyway, like it or not, which is why this book, unlike most management books, offers some precise and exact advice:

1. If you are not already using a high-powered personal computer or the equivalent, get one.
2. If you are, and it's not linked to any other computers in the organisation, find out the most effective and economical way of linking the whole outfit on a network.
3. Link it.
4. Accept thereafter that you will not manage the organisation as it has always been run – and act accordingly.
5. Manage the transition to the new system very deliberately to achieve precisely the results you want.
6. Accept that changes in circumstances and technology will necessitate and potentiate continuous change in the system – and act accordingly.

If you want to know why these six steps are necessary, and what benefits they will bring, read on.

BOOK I
The Shape of Things that Are

Chapter 1

The Technological Timebomb

In the spring of 1989, an assignment took me to the still-unfinished offices of an ambitious investment bank. Two vast floors had been filled with the highest of high technology, one floor for the traders in equity, the other for those dealing in debt. Some 300 identical desks were equipped with 300 identical sets of keyboards, screens and telephones. The decoration was mild enough on the eye, but functional and austere. In a few weeks' time, 300 non-identical human beings would be sitting at their identical work stations – and this would be the office of their futures, probably for as long as they cared to look ahead.

Their enormously expensive office, whose fitting out alone had cost £150 million, is not, fortunately, the office of everybody else's future. No area of modern life is undergoing so total a revolution as the office. In major part, the cause is technological: the technology which produces dehumanising results in the great trading rooms will have the opposite effect almost everywhere else. Every type of machine used in the office is being replaced by equipment that didn't exist before 1950 and that has powers to improve office life and effectiveness that were not even dimly envisaged at that time.

Like factory automation before it, technological revolution has come to the office just in time to avert crisis for industrial society – and post-industrial society, for that matter. The office is ubiquitous. Millions upon millions work in factories, mines, shops, ships, fields, schools and elsewhere. But behind and inside all these lies the office, housing still further millions who have never known another place of work. For many, the office is a home from home, often more home than home itself. Including travelling time, they may spend half their working days, perhaps three-quarters of their waking weekday hours, in this strange environment – one over which they have little power, and in which they can rarely exert much choice.

Look out from some midtown hotel in the United States, the

heartland of the office, as of industrial society generally, observe the blank walls of the skyscraper block opposite – where, even late at night, the odd lights burn – and you have to wonder about the quality of the life that goes on inside the towering, anonymous heights. When day comes, and the first workers arrive, the rituals begin: hanging up the coat, getting the first coffee, the talks across the desk, the first phone call. It's reminiscent of those nature films in which the micro-photographer peers inside the life of the hive.

In the explosive era of industrial civilisation, the insect analogy was more appropriate, although the animal analogy chosen was more often the bull. Office workers lived (for working is living) in "bull-pens", gigantic halls in which they occupied tiny desks and could be overseen by supervisors placed high above them. Old photographs of Victorian offices show the serried ranks of desks and people in mammoth rooms on which the sunlight seldom, if ever fell. It was at its worst in insurance offices in America – and the inhuman con-figuration, to judge by Billy Wilder's brilliant representation in *The Apartment*, was still common well into the period after the Second World War.

Wilder's hero, played by Jack Lemmon, escapes from the bullpen into the office worker's Nirvana: a room of his own. The true hier-archical divide in the traditional office is between those who have their own rooms and those forced to share. There are exceptions: merchant banks in the City of London, for example, were partnerships, and the partners would share a large room for reasons that were more practical than symbolic: each partner would know what the others were up to, and the exchange of information and advice was natural and easy.

By the same token, the single, walled office is more symbolic than practical. Its occupant can retreat into his fastness, close his door, shut out his colleagues. It symbolises privacy and the protection of secrets. In practical terms, it means that visits become more formal: whose office and at what time are questions that may have to be answered. Walk down the long corridors, with the nameplates outside each door, and the analogy is neither beehive nor bullpen, but a high-class prison: the main differences being that some inmates are not forced to share their cells and all are allowed home at night and weekends.

The pigeonhole principle needn't invalidate more open methods of working. In Japanese companies, the offices may be just as prison-like. Yet the principle of complementary skills and working in partnership is spread far more generally throughout the firm than usually holds in the West. The Japanese approach is culturally determined. But the fact that it is equally natural in the West is surely proved by the success, not only of long-term partnerships (which have been the foundation of many great Western businesses), but by the powerful survival, into the age of multi-national corporations, of family firms.

They are not commonly regarded as partnerships, but essentially a good and genuine family firm, like a good and genuine partnership, is a combination of complementary talents united by a common purpose and not divided by artificial lines of hierarchy or function. Such firms don't have an office culture: the culture is all-embracing, and the office is thus not separate from the rest of life, but part of the continuous interchange and comprehensive sharing that mark a successful partnership.

The working scene shifts from lunch-room to dinner at home, walks in the park to conference rooms, private offices to corridors. In firms which lack the unifying force of family or friendship, and which can't fall back on a Japanese-style culture of collaboration, physical devices may be required to move from pigeonhole to collaborative management. Open plans and glass dividers are obvious, if rarely successful examples. Some avant-garde managements have gone much further, seeking to stimulate a collegiate relationship by unusual means – like the brand-new Mid-Western steel company that built its office corridors especially wide to facilitate impromptu consultations.

There's an even more striking example, which, since it comes from Japan and from a company created by a famous two-man partnership, with financial and administrative acumen on one side and technological and marketing brilliance on the other, only emphasises the need for vigorous, deliberate pursuit of collaborative ends. At Honda, the senior executives jointly occupy an enormous room, where they also share symbolically round tables. Anybody who needs to start or join a discussion pulls up a chair; the chief executive himself has another round table in one of the corners.

As noted above, merchant banking partners in the City of London used to share rooms in a similar way. You can still find partners' desks, with kneeholes on four sides, that again symbolise a relationship that is coming to seem more and more essential as business becomes more complex. That may sound paradoxical: because when partners join forces, it's often in conditions of utmost simplicity (as in the proverbial garage). As the business grows and develops, the advent of more and more people must complicate the organisation and increase the demands on its management – notoriously, the most common cause of later failings, in partnerships and family firms alike, is failure to introduce new and needed management capacity and systems to match and sustain the growth of the business.

The most dangerous fault of successful managements is to take success, and the means that have created success, for granted. Most of the sore examples that have blighted corporate histories stem from this fundamental error: firms that were too slow to recognise that their traditional markets had vanished, Western factories that continued to use methods abandoned in Japan decades before, companies that missed the blatant significance of technological revolutions from the container to the semiconductor. But these failures of external perception are no less flagrant or harmful than internal blindness.

Procedures, systems and attitudes become set in granite, even though circumstances have radically changed. What is happening in the office has an analogy in the long process of acquisition, diversification and development that turns mono-product firms into multi-product combines. Often, the accounting systems don't evolve correspondingly. Consequently, the management, unable to tell where true profits and losses are being made, can't manage the whole intelligently. Promptly, that whole becomes worth much less than its parts. All managements, however, now face a common challenge, which is that the office environment they have known and mostly loved has become as obsolete as the one-track assembly line, the radio valve, or the old-style, pre-container docks.

The revolutionary potential of new equipment faces every office with the same challenge that Japanese methods have posed to Western factories. At the same time, the purposes of the office have changed in a way that is inimical to traditional organisation. The two forces are working in tandem: the new hardware and software make it possible, and in many respects essential, to change to the new methods of working, to shift away from the old office, which (like everything else in organisational life) is a product of historical accident. The offices which nearly all so-called white-collar workers (from chairmen to clerks) occupy are literally homes from home, houses in which each occupant has his or her space (from the chairman's suite to the clerk's desk).

Communication, before the telephone, either took place through exchanges of paper or face-to-face. The bullpen evolved partly for reasons of discipline, partly because more bodies could be packed into smaller space, but more importantly because the passage of paper and the spoken word is obviously eased by the absence of barriers and the proximity of desks – just as the traders, in the ultra-modern, high-tech bullpens, can yell at each other across the crowded room.

For those with work of higher degree, cacophony and lack of privacy were both demeaning and counter-productive. Like the Victorian father with his study, they had both dignity and high-level work to protect. So barriers (doors, walls, separate floors, even separate buildings) were erected to separate the barons from continuous direct contact with the commoners. Face-to-face discussion was still inevitable, indeed, vital; but the walls served to ration and limit the meetings, for which special rooms were supplied (right up to the holy of holies, the boardroom).

Thus the historic office developed, and thus it has largely remained. But now electronics offers the means for instantaneous communication and information anywhere in the company or anywhere in the world. This has happened at exactly the time when group working has of necessity replaced individual decision-making. Not only did the cellular office evolve for this one-man mode, but it powerfully reinforces the individual method of office work by isolating the office worker – and the higher the position, the greater the isolation.

Managers who don't recognise the potential of these developments will be like the failed companies of a frequently painful past: locked into ways of thought and action that will never cope with a fast-changing outside world. The pace of technological advance is so frenetic that the full extent of the revolution cannot be predicted. But hardware or software already exists, or lies round a near corner, that will perform any task currently done in offices much faster, more conveniently, more accurately; and many tasks which now can't be done at all will become routine.

The revolution is of a wholly different order of magnitude from the slow changes of the twentieth century. The technology of the office of the past has seen five major and crucial developments: the telephone and its printed allies, the telex and the ticker tape; the typewriter; the copier; the adding machine and its replacement, the electronic calculator; and the computer. The first three represented new and vastly improved methods of conducting business as before. The post and the personal meeting were no longer the sole means of communication. Laborious and slow longhand was replaced by the sometimes amazingly fast typist. Her skills, in turn, were supplemented by the far greater speeds of the xerographic copier.

Like the phone, the typewriter and the copier, the computer, in its first use as a glorified adding machine, produced an enormous enhancement of existing processes. The new electronic technology, however, makes new processes not only possible, but inevitable. The most exciting aspect of the office revolution is the impact that new technology will have on the process of management itself. But a less glamorous example of the sweeping changes ahead already exists in EDI – electronic data interchange. Firms can now give and take orders, and supply and pay for the goods, without any paper changing hands, without any direct human intervention, and with automatic bookkeeping for the transactions. It is a whole New World, and like the inhabitants of Europe when the Americas opened up, nobody living and working in an office will be untouched by the culture shock to come.

Chapter 2

THE OFFICE OF THE PRESENT – AND FUTURE

In March 1989, *Wall Street Journal* reporter Carol Hymowitz put together a day in the life of a fictitious American executive. It offered a fascinating, personalised glimpse of what is happening in the executive suite – and in the executive home:

6.10 a.m. ... and another Monday morning has begun for Peter Smith. The marketing vice-president for the home-appliance division of a major US manufacturer is awakened by his computer alarm. He saunters to his terminal to check the weather outlook in Madrid, where he'll fly late tonight, and to send an electronic-voice message to a supplier in Thailand.

7.20 a.m. Mr Smith and his wife, who heads her own architecture firm, organise the home front... They leave instructions for their personal computer to call the home-cleaning service as well as a gourmet carry-out service that will prepare dinner for eight guests Saturday. And they quickly go over the day's schedules for their three- and six-year old daughters with their nanny. On the train ... Mr Smith checks his electronic mailbox and also reads his favourite trade magazine via his lap-top computer.

8.15 a.m. In his high-tech office that doubles as a conference room, Mr Smith reviews the day's schedule with his executive assistant (traditional secretaries [have] vanished...). Then it's on to his first meeting: a conference via video between his division's chief production manager in Cincinnati and a supplier near Munich.

The supplier tells them she can deliver a critical component for a new appliance at a 10% cost saving if they grab it within a week. Mr Smith and the production manager quickly concur that it's a good deal. While they'll have to immediately change production schedules, they'll be able to snare a new customer who has been balking about price.

10.30 a.m. At a staff meeting Mr Smith finds himself refereeing between two subordinates who disagree vehemently on how to promote a new appliance. One, an Asian manager, suggests that a fresh campaign begin much sooner than initially envisioned. The other, a European, wants to hold off until results of a test market are received later that week.

Mr Smith quickly realises that this is a cultural, not strategic clash, pitting a let's-do-it-now, analyse-it-later approach against a more cautious style. He makes them aware they're not really far apart and the European manager agrees to move swiftly.

12.30 p.m. Lunch is in Mr Smith's office today, giving him time to take a video lesson in conversational Chinese. He already speaks Spanish fluently, learned during a work stint in Argentina, and wants to master at least two more languages. After twenty minutes, though, he decides to go to his computer to check his company's latest political risk-assessment on Spain, where recent student unrest has erupted into riots. The report tells him that the disturbances aren't anti-American, but he decides to have a bodyguard meet him at the Madrid airport, anyway.

2.20 p.m. Two of Mr Smith's top lieutenants complain that they and others on his staff feel a recent bonus payment for a successful project wasn't divided equitably. Bluntly, they note that while Mr Smith received a hefty $20,000 bonus, his fifteen-member staff had to split $5,000, and they threaten to defect. He quickly calls his boss, who says he'll think about increasing the bonus for staff members.

4 p.m. Mr Smith learns from the field that a large retail customer has been approached by a foreign competitor promising to quickly supply him with a best-selling appliance. After conferring with this division's production managers, he phones the customer and suggests that his company could supply the same product but with three slightly different custom designs. They arrange a meeting later in the week.

6 p.m. Before heading to the airport, Mr Smith uses his video phone to give his daughters a goodnight kiss and to talk about the next day's schedule with his wife. Learning that she must take an unex-

pected trip herself the next evening, he promises to catch the Super-
Concorde home in time to put the kids to sleep himself.

The most fascinating aspect of this day-in-the-life-of, given away
by "the Super-Concorde" and the video phone, is that it is set in the
future: not the near future, but the far distance of 2010, two decades
on from the date of the article. Yet almost every one of the other
technological wonders described either exists and operates right now
(even the "electronic voice message" or the PC that can pass on
messages) or is in an advanced state of development. Indeed, the pace
of development is so fast that, by the time these words are read, the
whole of Mr Smith's armoury could be commercially available.

A typical page in *Business Week*, published a few months after Peter
Smith's day, records a facsimile machine that plugs into a laser printer
(thus greatly improving output quality); the impending arrival of a
"Hypercube" for offices to enable many microprocessors, by splitting
work between them in so-called parallel processing, to outperform
both minis and mainframes in handling large databases; and a word
processing program to enlarge computer screen type for the benefit of
screen-squinters – all wonders that are relatively established.

That is only the tip of the iceberg of the development pace and
effort now going into enhancing the existing technology, creating
wholly new possibilities and removing the last roadblocks in the path
of the revolutionary army. The obstinacy of the non-human barriers
to change shouldn't be underestimated, true. An expert on relational
database management systems, Oracle's John Spiers, had this to say
in the summer of 1989 about "distributed DBMS and hence, fully
distributed applications systems" (i.e., anybody anywhere in the
company can run any and all of the programs that anybody else is
using).

These, Spiers wrote, "are the 'promised land' of information technology, but the fact has to be faced that at the moment the supporting
technology is not sufficiently developed to provide the functionality,
manageability, speed and reliability that networked systems require".
Nobody doubts, however, that the non-human barriers will be and
are being overcome: we'll get to the promised land. The human barriers
have retarded progress infinitely more than the technical ones. Even
Carol Hymowitz missed an opportunity that today's Peter Smith, let
alone 2010's, has at his disposal. The bonus system, for instance, could
be a carefully worked out scheme, available for inspection via the
computer for all affected, which would instantly confirm (or otherwise)
the fairness of the bonus.

If, nevertheless, there was a dispute, those concerned, Smith, the latter's boss and the aggrieved parties, could settle it at once, all looking at the same details on their separate screens. That is today's technology. But even those who have its basic element, personal computing, don't exploit it to anything like the full potential. Quite recent studies showed that users of the dominant MS/DOS technology (more commonly known as IBM-compatible) only used an average four programs out of the many thousands available, while their machines were only worked for half an hour a day.

That technical barriers lay behind this low usage seems to emerge clearly from statistics for the only rival technology: seven programs and three and a half hours of use for Apple Macintoshes. The comparisons have to be approached cautiously, since the population of MS/DOS computers in offices is vastly larger than that of Apple Macs, and it may be that, relatively and absolutely, far fewer Macs were foisted on reluctant users. But these PCs do offer precisely the ease-of-use advantages which the researchers at Palo Alto, working for Xerox Corporation, identified as essential long ago.

These are the graphical interface, using icons and symbols as user guides; the "mouse" pointer to replace keyboard instructions; and the consistency of the user interface – so that the same graphics and the same commands operate in the same way for all programs. There's no room left for argument about which of the competing technologies has the advantage in these respects, since MS/DOS suppliers are gravitating at various speeds to the graphical layouts, mouse or similar controls and standard user interfaces that Palo Alto foresaw long ago.

The ease-of-use issue has been the Achilles' heel of the IT industry. But coming and totally certain developments in technology, building on the advance represented by the pull-down menu and the mouse, will end the era of user-hostility, and not before time. Congratulating your computer for being "user-friendly" is a nonsense in itself. It suggests that making a hard-to-use product is some kind of acceptable norm. Car makers make much the same error when boasting that their machines are "safe". Nobody would buy a car that wasn't supposedly safe, and nobody would buy a computer (any more than a car) that wasn't "user-friendly": unless they had no option.

Computing is now generally becoming friendlier; but meanwhile another trend is working towards the preservation of complexity. New generations of schoolchildren are emerging from education used to computers, and handling the awkwardnesses of the MS/DOS world with the nonchalant ease of somebody who has been taught to play the piano. Indeed, Peter Drucker once suggested that musical notation might provide the key to the computer age – that a computer language, as easy to learn as music, could become the *lingua franca* of the electronic revolution.

The *lingua franca*, it is now clear, will be ordinary language, above all English. There's no point in sticking to complex ways of operating machines when simple English commands – provided by pointers, typed in or vocalised – will do the job. Equally, though, it will become unnecessary to make concessions to keyboard-shy executives: to supply executive information systems, for example, where buttons, rather than typed commands, summon up the statistics. The present generation of managers will be succeeded by a race of Peter Smiths, with one computer at home, another in the briefcase, a third in the executive work station in the office, and all three able to communicate and work easily with the others.

Certain consequences flow, however, from the increase in power that will give the next generation of executive work stations ten times the capacity of the products of the late 1980s. The power explosion makes it possible to eliminate another user-hostile feature: the fact that new programs have to be learnt with cumbersome manuals supplemented by expensive courses. Self-teaching programs will use algorithmic methods to instruct users as they actually work with the application: the answers to queries and problems will be in the disc, not the manual – a dinosaur-like survival into the electronic age when a Peter Smith *might* read a magazine via a screen.

The word "might" is italicised because flicking through printed material is a very fast way of searching when readers don't know what they are seeking – so the eye can be caught by a headline, a subject, or a photograph. Electronic "reading" must win when the search is for something specific – details of a contract in Saudi Arabia, a remembered article on the latest advances in electronic point of sale, an ad for new software, or whatever. That apart, the power of electronics works, not against, but in tandem with publishing – on the desktop.

Even in the world of office automation, few technologies have caught on so rapidly as desktop publishing. It follows on logically from the software that, able to handle both data and documents, is basic to true Office Systems Technology. Large screens make it possible to view a number of electronic documents simultaneously, while colour and the computer's remarkable skills as draughtsman make presentation far more effective as images, graphics and text enhance and expand the figures.

With DTP, the compound document on the screen can be swiftly presented, for internal and external use, as "hard copy". Reports and recommendations come to life in ways that, because they are unfamiliar, will take time to be established. But, like most of Peter

Smith's paraphernalia for the year 2010, DTP was working with perfect and popular effectiveness in 1989. The issue is rapidly becoming not whether to install DTP, but which system to use, and for what purposes.

That sentence applies as strongly to the electronic office as a whole. As the decade ended, few executives believed that they had truly achieved effective use of such office systems as they possessed. Despite growing awareness of the value of information, including its strategic use, companies have manifestly found it very difficult to gain the full value from an IT investment which mounted massively during the 1980s. The reasons are buried deep in the changing structure of business and management, and the solution lies in the marriage of those fundamental changes to the new powers of the technology. Every day brings that wedding inevitably nearer.

Chapter 3

THE OFFICE OF THE PAST – AND PRESENT

The rise in the proportion of so-called white-collar workers no longer needs charting: like the rising of the sun, it is a dominant, inescapable fact of life. "White-collar" and "blue-collar", of course, have long since ceased to be accurate divisions. A better division (though itself rapidly becoming obsolete) is between those who work in offices and those who don't. And it's clear that the number of office workers is likely to continue mounting at a pace that puts increasing pressure on the economics of the firm.

Between 1971 and 1986, according to the Warwick Institute for Employment Research, white-collar workers in the UK moved into the majority: their numbers rose from 10 million to over 12 million while the blue-collar force fell from 14 million to under 12 million. A significant part of this decline lay in the decimation of British manufacturing in the early Thatcher years, followed by the continuing swing towards rationalisation of production, both by concentrating output on fewer plants and by automating operations within the factories.

The latter process is worldwide, and so is the rise of the service industries. These trends suggest that by 1995 British white-collar work will occupy as many people as the blue-collars of 1971, with the whites leading the blues by 2 million. A survey commissioned from the Henley Centre by the Satex Group notes that "While the first industrial revolution was driven by the move from a primarily agriculturally-based to an industrially-based society, the current one reflects the move into a post-industrial or information-based society, where the majority are employed in jobs which process information – such as clerks, secretaries, stockbrokers, lawyers, bankers and technicians."

The report goes on to point out that "All these are office-based jobs", and that "the ongoing expansion in employment in the business services sector" is the primary engine of the white-collar revolution. An accompanying chart, also from the Warwick Institute, shows that all the net increase in employment foreseen between 1986 and 1995 will be the result of the 1.4 million gain expected in "business and miscellaneous services"; elsewhere, declines in manufacturing and primary production will be offset by small advances in construction, non-marketed services, distribution and transport.

The broad figures are clearly based on painstaking and accurate analysis. But they conceal as much as they reveal. The processing of information undertaken by clerks and secretaries is of a different order from that of bankers and technicians – not to mention managers. Many people employed in "services", moreover, are doing work (such as fast-food processing) which represents no significant advance over assembly line labour. The overall numbers ignore the fact that the white-blue colour or collar shift is being matched inside organisations by a trend of equal importance – the decline of people employed in the operational, clerical functions (the "clerks, secretaries"), and the rise of information workers, as opposed to mere processors.

The latter group must continue to reduce in numbers as information systems take over more and more of the "structured" activities; tasks which can be shaped in advance, and taught by rote, and which never vary significantly. At the same time the number of management staff and professionals working on the "unstructured" needs will continue to swell. Unstructured tasks cannot be taught by rote, vary continually, and shape themselves as they progress. They fall to executives, professional staff, and knowledge workers. Increasingly, the office will become a machine for their use.

If their numbers were to rise more slowly than the number of structured jobs falls, the economic pressure on organisations would lessen. Its principal form (but not the only one) is the cost of physical space. Between 1987 and 1988, according to Hillier Parker, office rentals in the south-east of England rose by 35%. The rise in the City and the West End of London has been faster still – 45% in central districts in the year to April 1987. When a Japanese company bought the *Financial Times* building in the City, its staggering price of £143 million implied a rent of £70 a square foot. A modest office of 100 square feet thus makes the expense of employing a fairly junior executive £7,000 a year before any service and maintenance costs – let alone salary and fringe benefits.

The knock-on effect on the economy at large must be enormous – when a sizeable firm of solicitors has £17 million of occupancy costs to cover before earning any money for its staff, the steep rise in legal fees becomes much easier to understand. In theory, in any market, rising prices choke off demand, partly by discouraging potential buyers and partly by encouraging over-supply. The latter tendency has been apparent in both Britain and the US, where F. W. Dodge, Inc, reported 1.6 billion square feet of construction contracts for investment-grade office space in the mid-eighties.

The corresponding figure for 1971–79 was 600 million square feet. In London, in the autumn of 1987, 17 million square feet of new space were being planned – such was the confidence, before the stock market crash that October, that demand for modern, high-technology offices would be insatiable. The cycle of shortage creating price rises creating surplus must have some effect. Before the decade ended, a decentralising movement out of the dearer areas had already begun. But the rental rise elsewhere has also been steep: the south-west comfortably exceeded the south-east in 1988, while fringe areas near the City of London have seen rises of up to 70%.

But price isn't the only factor retarding escape from the high-rent areas. Resistance to decentralisation, or its mirror image, clinging to centralisation, has powerful non-economic causes. In investigating the potential for home-working (which is another escape route), the Henley Centre explains that "Occupation remains highly important in defining how people view their status in society and their relationship with others. And as the physical interaction with other people in the workplace is an important aspect of this self-definition, they are unlikely to want to be isolated from it on a permanent basis." By the same token, working in a "prestigious" office in a city centre is an important aspect of the self-definition of an executive in a major organisation.

So far as home-working is concerned, Henley believes that in consequence its full-time use will be rare even in 1995 – no more than 390,000 potential homeworkers against almost 12 million who would be willing to work at home for some of the time. It argues that part-timers will still need full-time office space: hence the expectation of a continued high level of demand for offices both centrally and away from the centre – "administration and clerical" activities, which "consistently take up between one-fifth and one-third of space", will increasingly be relocated to cheaper areas.

That will leave "the core staff involved in policy, decision-making and client liaison" in the central locations. In other words, the "structured" jobs will move out, while the "unstructured" workers, from the chief executive to the computer programmer, stay in the expensive space. This suggests that two types of office will emerge: one very similar to the office of the past, a beehive for the workers; the other a highly flexible, high-technology environment where the emphasis is on adding value.

At £70 a square foot, there really is no option. One of the prime unstructured tasks, indeed, will be to ensure that the productivity of unstructured workers is sufficient to justify their occupancy costs. In many cases, the objective will be unattainable. Since the tasks still have to be done, sub-contracting of unstructured knowledge work seems certain to rise. Another factor is that the diminishing population of young people will force up the price of those (mainly graduates) who can tackle unstructured work: and the population trends are both inexorable and powerful, according to United Nations figures.

Between 1985 and 2000, the population of 18 to 23-year-olds is expected to fall by 44% in West Germany, a quarter in both Italy and the UK, and 13% in France and the United States. As the Satex report says, "it is clear that the increasing expense of hiring staff will force the issue of sub-contracting of white-collar services much further up the management agenda." It must have already occupied quite a high position in 1988, when the Arbitration and Conciliation Service found that 40% of companies were increasingly using sub-contractors, and 18% had plans to do so.

Some of these services may be clerical and administrative, which is a long-established practice – computer bureaux have been handling payroll for customers since near the start of the computer era. But well before 1990 the proliferation of sub-contractors handling key *unstructured* tasks had become a highly prominent feature of the Western world. Take this random selection of services offered by "sole practitioners and practising firms" belonging to the Institute of Management Consultants in 1989:

> Business and marketing strategy and planning ... achieving inno-
> vation, improving communication and team-working ... overhead
> cost appraisals ... validating market projections ... career coun-
> selling, succession planning, staff and candidate assessment and
> appraisal ... production planning and control ... economic, finan-
> cial and management information services ... organising, develop-
> ing and motivating people as the key to strategy implementation
> ... best world practices in strategy development, managing
> change, cost reduction, customer service and profit enhancement.

That selection was truly random – the result of casually opening a reference book and quoting from the first page to appear. These are not the large multi-national consultancies, either, but small firms, sometimes one-man operations. Yet their claims for services rendered cover the whole gamut of management, across all functions and from the boardroom to the shop floor. These, moreover, are relative generalists. Other armies of highly skilled people provide specific services ranging from largely non-technical areas like recruitment and its opposite, "out-placement", to the extremes of sophistication in technological consultancy.

The higher that in-house costs mount, and the greater the difficulty of recruiting and retaining the best people, the more attractive sub-contracted or consultancy fees will seem. Moreover, just as no company, however large and rich, can now maintain world-class capability in all relevant technologies, so no management can provide, from within its own ranks, world-class capability in all relevant disciplines. The alternative is to find a world-class external specialist who can supply the expertise – and who can be far more easily replaced if the service proves to be inadequate.

These services, what's more, may not need to carry the burden of heavy rental overheads (which, initially, are the supplier's problem, not the customer's). The random list above was gleaned from firms working as far apart as Dublin, Teddington, Hertfordshire, Sydenham, Croydon, Cork and Warwick: only one operated in an expensive London area, Kensington. Because of the speed of modern communications, including jet travel, the whole world has become open to the sub-contracting management. The jet-set management consultant has become an everyday reality, following his speciality wherever it leads.

The offices of such sub-contractors themselves are having to lead the way into the future. Wherever they are, the consultants have to keep in touch with base and with widespread clients. They experience in an acute form the varied challenges that face all unstructured knowledge workers. They get input from a whole range of sources, including internal and external databases. A myriad of reports come across their desks. They have to gain effective access to the information available, and they have to assimilate it. In addition, they need to take views from other people and then communicate their ideas.

Finally, they have to initiate, supervise, monitor and modify action. They operate in a world where multiple locations are the norm. Even if a company can concentrate its core activities on one site, its customers may well be spread across several regions, countries or both. In earlier, simpler times this mattered little, because customer relations were neither seen nor treated as a source of competitive advantage. Today and tomorrow, the truth that the customer is the company will be rammed home time and again in the marketplace.

The multi-location, multi-function management will increasingly come to resemble the consultants upon whose services it calls – highly experienced specialists who are constantly on the move, both between locations, and between "clients": in the corporate case "clients" includes different working groups inside the company who are dealing with different aspects of its affairs where the particular specialist has a unique contribution to make – but where that contribution only reaches its full value via group working.

This sounds like science fiction by the norms of the eighties. The fact is that during the decade the earlier revolution in hardware was rounded off by one in software – but only to the extent of making the machines workable and useful. The basic "software" elements (so to speak) of the office itself are the uses to which it is put, and they have barely changed throughout the revolution in machines. It's as if today's highly mechanised car factories were being used to manufacture Model Ts. The historic office is the present office: a place where people are brought together under one roof for reasons, and to perform tasks, that belong to the past, but not necessarily to the present – still less the future.

The shape of things to come, however, is clear. Like the consultant of today, the manager of tomorrow will be permanently on the move. But the key to the revolution is that managers, if they wish, can be peripatetic without ever leaving their city centre offices; or central to the company's success without ever entering those sacred portals.

Chapter 4

THE NEW OFFICE WORKERS

The shape of the office of tomorrow is not difficult to determine, because it exists today. Major organisations only have to follow the example of some minor outfits – notably the same consultancies mentioned in the previous chapter, where the "output" largely consists of thought and information, and where the nature of the work has long since forced the workers into the necessary mode. These companies are already what Charles Handy, author of *The Age of Unreason*, has identified as "shamrock" organisations, referring to the three-leaved Irish national emblem.

His first leaf consists of the people who are truly indispensable to the organisation – who in a sense *are* the organisation. This core "is increasingly made up of qualified professionals, technicians and managers" (the very same people as those identified by Peter Drucker, in his discussion of the same phenomenon, as "specialists"). Between them, says Handy, the core employees "own the organisational knowledge which distinguishes the organisation from its counterparts. Lose them and you lose some of yourself." These precious and hard-to-replace people are also hard to get, and their numbers are reducing as their price is rising.

Handy points to the disappearance, on Conference Board figures, of more than a million managers and staff professionals in the United States between 1979 and 1983. Many of these may not have been true core workers, in Handy's own definition. But the point is well taken: tomorrow's core will be smaller than today's, and will manage on its reduced numbers by increasingly heavy use of the second leaf of the shamrock – contracted-out key services. Whatever the proportion of work placed outside – Handy thinks it may already be 80% in some cases – the global village has spread this new form of cottage industry worldwide, with Singapore, for example, becoming a printing and distribution centre for publishers based 8,000 miles away.

Francis Kinsman, author of *The Telecommuters* (a title that refers to people who don't commute from home to work, but whose work commutes to them through information technology), has written in *Finance* magazine that "American Airlines is already running its entire ticketing operation from Barbados", while "In China, a Californian company is now flying in data for entry and onward satellite transmission to Australia". He notes that, as the second leaf of the shamrock continues to grow, "many managers in the next century will be faced with the facts of ferociously competitive international telecommuting" – whether they like it or not.

The third leaf is something that managers evidently do like – "the flexible labour force, all those part-time workers and temporary workers who are the fastest growing part of the employment scene". Plainly, the modern service economy could not run without the availability of staff to meet peak demand at economic cost. In fact, the trend may well be towards *permanent* part-time staff: you could redefine Handy's shamrock metaphor, dividing it between the core, the sub-contractors, and the interface – meaning all the people, full-time and part-time, who intermediate between the planners, designers and decision-makers in the core and the customers outside the organisation, without whom it would rapidly cease to exist.

However it is defined, the shamrock will be unified by the power of electronics. Inevitably, to use Handy's phrase, the electronic shamrock will involve "a new concept of the central office". He tells of visiting a typical office of today (or yesterday) in central London. "The chief executive was thinking of re-designing the floor layout to allow, he said, for more informal interaction between his executives, for more meeting rooms and rooms dedicated to particularly expensive pieces of electronic hardware."

For such purposes, "the present layout of rooms as rows, or rather layers and layers ... of individual offices" is plainly unsuitable. But Handy noticed something else: in this case, the offices were empty: it turned out that the executives were all away on business, and only came in to file reports, attend departmental meetings or deal with their correspondence. As Handy pointed out, while the cost per executive of city centre office housing is high enough, the cost of actual *occupancy* must be grotesquely extravagant.

He offered his host an alternative vision; the visionary company concerned, one of the consultancy-type organisms mentioned in the first paragraph, is anonymous in Handy's book, but is easily identifiable as Wolff Olins, co-founded by one of my own oldest friends. Starting from democratic rather than utilitarian principles, Wally Olins has built a design consultancy from small beginnings to relatively large scale on an open-plan, free-form style. Nobody has a private office; secretaries are truly personal assistants; people come and go as their work demands; and an excellent, heavily subsidised restaurant is maintained in the basement. Handy quotes our mutual friend's definition: "It's a working club, really."

The metaphor is a good one, since it points to the dangers, as well as the great potential, of this type of office organisation. Companies that become too clubby, too much of a home from home, are as likely to become inbred and unresponsive to challenge and change as the old dinosaur bureaucracies. Running shamrock organisations requires clear lines of responsibility, exacting relationships with sub-contractors and continuously improved direction of the workers at the interface: and none of that can be achieved without the discipline of managed information.

It follows that managing information flows, not managing the office, becomes the prime administrative responsibility. The "management information services" (MIS) department, or whatever else it is called, has the responsibility for arranging to provide the facts and figures required by management, in the form in which they are most useful, and for co-ordinating all the separate requirements of all core professionals into a coherent, economic whole.

It isn't a function which is well performed, if performed at all, in perhaps all organisations today. Talk to MIS managers in the most information-dependent corporations, like banks or oil companies, and you hear horror stories of overlaps, incompatibilities and competing systems. The rapid rise of CASE (computer assisted systems engineering), however, shows that this uncoordinated sprawl belongs to the past, not the future. Using CASE programs, companies can build a hierarchy of mutually reinforcing competences, leading up to an integrated system of decision support.

All this, though, will be unseen in the revolutionary office. The managed systems will work as swiftly and silently away as the familiar airline reservation tools. The small management teams, drawn from different disciplinary backgrounds, but united by long experience of group working, will operate in spaces of more open design which can easily accommodate a culture of continual "meetings" – only they will not be formal meetings as known today, but more like the rehearsal sessions of jazz musicians.

These informal and informally led groupings will be cloned right down an organisation where hierarchy has no operational role and special skills are dominant – no matter who wields them. The secretarial and other support staff will still be there, but in smaller numbers, and there will be fewer offices. Like the one Handy visited, these will often seem to be empty: simply because the executive's "office" will be wherever he or she has to be. The "boss", the *primus inter pares*, will care little about their whereabouts at any particular time – no more than the political secretaries who governed India in the days of the British Raj (which has provided Peter Drucker with some fascinating analogies) knew the location of any particular district officer among their subordinates.

The whereabouts of the chief executive himself may not matter to any greater degree. In July 1989, the *Financial Times* commented that "Mr Robert Evans has not been discomfited by the recent transport strikes. He works from home. He has a computer, a facsimile machine, a printer and a telephone system, and he types his own letters. What makes this unusual is that he is not a self-employed businessman but chief executive of a public company" – and possibly the very first, anywhere in the world, to free himself from the office entirely.

That might seem to follow quite logically from the fact that the company, Systems Reliability Holdings, is engaged in activities like selling microcomputers, reconfiguring IBM computers, telephone management and personalised answering systems. But Evans is an accountant by background, not an information technology specialist, and his previous experience was in the food business. It's interesting that his only problem in assembling a home office was "to assemble the various electronic gadgets . . . from the myriad potential suppliers".

The opportunity he thus spotted was to assemble the gadgets in one package, so as to offer the executives of the future the "home management kit". The odds are overwhelming that, by the time executives of the future catch up with the technology of today, stand-alone units will have generally given way to comprehensive, integrated work stations that can operate equally well in the office or the home: in either location, the workstations will be integrated with the entire information apparatus of the organisation.

What's sauce for the chief executive gander is sauce for the subordinate goose. Writing in *Finance* magazine in the autumn of 1988, Francis Kinsman recounted how "Five years ago Rank Xerox UK was shaken to find that in central London it was doling out something like two and a half times an individual's salary for associated costs such as office rent, rates and upkeep, secretarial assistance, company car, pension, sick pay, and the usual range of perks." The answer was to detach people in activities as varied "as pension fund administration, fleet car purchasing, and personnel consultancy".

The company met its own needs by letting these "networks" leave the company and rehiring them at once as freelance consultants who devoted up to half their time to serving Rank Xerox "at a rate that maximised at about their usual basic salary – but without the costly fringe benefits". For the rest of their time, the networkers were free to work for other clients. At the time Kinsman wrote, none out of sixty "networks" had failed – after being trained by their former employer, note, not only in entrepreneurial techniques, but, vitally, in microcomputing skills.

In 1990, the number of professional managers employed in major organisations who are skilled in either department represents a small minority. If the minority is not a majority by the year 2000, it will surely be computerate (standing for computer-literate) not long after the century turns. Schoolchildren are now acquiring computeracy along with the other basic skills of numeracy and literacy, and enhancing them through the playing of business games. Not only must the dream of a computer on every executive desk become reality, but homes with books will also be homes with as many computers as they now have stereo systems.

In this environment, whether executives work at home (like Robert Evans), in the office "club", or away from both will have little significance. Ironically, the out-of-office life has long been routine for supposedly lesser breeds like salespeople. In pragmatic companies, these itinerants have neither offices nor desks, but lockable cabinets on castors. When they have to return to base, for meetings, paperwork or whatever, they roll the cabinet over to any vacant desk and start work, using the hardware (probably only a typewriter and a telephone) that sits on the "workstation".

The computer provides the exact equivalent of the locked, luggable filing cabinet. With his electronic files, the executive can sit down at any desk anywhere inside the office or inside the company or outside both and begin work. At present, Kinsman's telecommuters and the corporate executive seem like different breeds, and Evans like some kind of eccentric. In future, telecommuting will seem no stranger than commuting does now: like facsimile and CASE, what once seemed curiosities becomes everyday reality with astonishing speed in the end-century environment.

Kinsman's rules for successful telecommuting, in fact, fit remarkably well with Peter Drucker's essentials for success in the information-based organisation (see Chapters 11 and 12). "First," writes Kinsman, "the mission, the corporate vision, must be paramount and clear. Everybody must know the organisation's aim and his or her part in its framework." He affirms that "distributed organisations have to be both flexible and highly formalised, with extremely precise assessment, monitoring, and estimating procedures."

Within this information structure, "individuals are empowered to carry out their tasks in whatever way suits them." Instead of Handy's shamrock, Kinsman offers as metaphor the "organisation sponge", which has "semi-autonomous interdependent units connected together by the matrix which roots them and forming a structure with a softer outline within which they operate and which in turn they nourish by their activities".

Team-building, moreover, "has to be engendered far more specifically than with a traditional organisation. Participation of all kinds, feedback on assessment of output, and a sense of fun and excitement are the three elements of this." What's true of telecommuting self-evidently applies to all management. Work in the office revolution has no necessary shape, and its nature is to be free-form. That being so, offices are free to take whatever shape and form their occupants like – and that is what will happen.

Chapter 5

THE STRUCTURE OF THE OFFICE

Does the office need to exist at all? Could there be an equivalent to the "hollow corporation" – a marketing company that sells manufactured, branded products without having any manufacturing facilities of its own? The equivalent, to carry on the theme of the previous chapter, would be a company whose officers never met, communicating only by electronic devices, kept fully in touch with each other's activities and thoughts by their shared workstations, and working wherever in the country, or indeed the world, that they preferred.

The situation sounds fantastical. But eccentrics do exist in the here and now who not only work in isolation, but do so from deliberate choice. In the pre-electronic era, there was a Wall Street sage who locked himself away in a windowless room, bereft of any means of communication with the outside world, in order to reach his investment decisions free of any outside influence. Deep into the electronic age, Elaine Garzarelli, the latter-day guru who rose to instant fame by correctly calling the imminent advent of the crash of '87, did likewise.

She has no company save her electronic tools during the two weeks every month when she analyses her quantitative data (she is a leading light of the so-called "quants", who go entirely by statistics). Certainly, the office revolution will get more such choices – more people who, while not going so far as Garzarelli, will imitate Warren Buffett; the only person ever to have made a billion dollars by straight qualitative investment, he operates from Omaha, Nebraska, as distant as possible from the hectic atmosphere of both East and West Coasts. Yet what makes those atmospheres hectic is the fact that the above eccentrics *are* eccentric. Other human beings generally prefer to congregate, to "eyeball" each other, to "press the flesh", to rub shoulders, to wallow in gossip.

To stay with the investment world, many in the City of London now believe that it was a mistake to abandon the trading floor of the

Stock Exchange for the impersonal, anonymous screen, reckoning that face-to-face contact on the floor would have produced more orderly market conditions during the critical autumn days of 1987. Certainly, traders in the days before financial deregulation wouldn't have been able to break contact by the somewhat reprehensible method available to the new market-makers. When the heat got too intense, it's alleged, some simply didn't answer their phones.

That goes to the heart of the person-to-person issue. In theory, there is no business that cannot be transacted to perfect satisfaction by phone, letter, telex, facsimile, electronic messaging, or, if more than two people are involved, by hook-ups: the wondrous new technology of teleconferencing, which allows the participants to see the face as well as hear the voice, is bound to expand. Already, the vast bulk of the world's business is conducted by such impersonal means. Lifelong relationships can be established between people who have never met, even in the same company. Even the latter is likely to become much more dispersed – as noted in Chapter 4, the fully employed tele-commuter, who uses the new technology to work from home and never needs to go near the office, is already a reality.

It must be far more economic to move the work to the people than the people to the work. That being so, both the teleconference and the telecommuter are bound to rise, probably at an exponential rate, over the coming years, and the genuine "*tele*phone", adding the other party's face to the conversation, will with equal inevitability advance from science fiction into everyday fact. Yet it's much too early to start dumping airline shares. The incessant business traffic on which all airlines depend for their survival is almost bound to continue its inexorable advance – certainly if the Japanese have anything to do with it.

Old Far East hands advise that doing significant business in Japan is impossible unless your top man meets their top man. Phone calls won't do: the relationship must be established personally, however irksome the journey to the other side of the world. The other way round, the Japanese are insatiable business travellers. To observers or participants in the typical encounter, conducted through an interpreter and stilted, not only for that reason, but because of the cultural differences, the human value when East meets West may not be immediately obvious. But to the Japanese, the phrase "It's not what you know, it's who you know" has special meaning: he is unhappy unless he *knows* the person with whom he is dealing – and that means seeing, hearing, sensing, entertaining, conversing.

Western politicians have much the same penchant. Chancellor Kohl of West Germany does not, one may safely assume, count as lost the hours not spent in the company of Mrs Thatcher, and she, in turn, has never counted the days until their next unloving encounter. But when political business has to be conducted between the two countries, such leaders jump into their limousines and aircraft to discuss face-to-face the issues which have no doubt previously been masticated over to the last morsel by their officials. It doesn't matter: just as with Soviet–American summits, the contact is seen to be as important as the content – which in most such cases has all been decided well in advance.

That isn't the case with most business meetings. Indeed, their beset-ting sin is lack of sufficient preparation. Directors arrive in the board-room with little idea about what is going to be discussed, let alone decided. Executive information systems are already beginning to make such sloppiness a thing of the past. In such loose circumstances, personality is often decisive in swaying opinion, for good or (very often) for ill. But personality is always a major influence in what the innocent might suppose is the entirely rational conduct of business affairs. That's why nobody would dream of appointing somebody even to a minor job without the candidate being interviewed face-to-face. Nobody thinks they know enough about people until they have seen them and talked to them in the flesh.

Whether the job interview is as important as employers suppose is another matter: its conduct is generally abysmal, and the success rate of arranged marriages and mail order brides is probably no lower than that of most corporate appointments. Here, too, computerised matching of job requirements with candidates will become a routine part of the office revolution. But it's perfectly natural and right to take strangers literally at face value, if only because their physical presence – their voice, their look, their looks, their dress – will have a profound effect on your attitude towards them, and thus on their effectiveness, after they join the firm.

But why should what applies to strangers have any bearing on people you already know well? Why must the head of a division journey all the way from Winnipeg or Wigan to confer with a chief executive who has been a close acquaintance for all their joint working lives? Custom and habit obviously play some part. But deep human needs are more significant. Business is a highly social activity. People don't only work to make money: they crave the company of the company, so to speak.

The human contacts – the board meetings, the impromptu con-ferences, the business lunches, the head round the office door – are dearly prized aspects of office existence, and their absence is probably the hardest loss the retired executive, or the transplanted homeworker, has to bear. A voice at the other end of a phone cannot supply these social needs, which are not, in any event, purposeless. The corporate culture determines the corporate potential, and that culture is created by the human contacts of the people inside the organisation.

But there's more to the necessity of contact than social or cultural requirements. "Face-to-face" (and still more "eyeball to eyeball") has a strong suggestion of confrontation. This is the human animal squaring up to another, maybe in a friendly manner, maybe not – not at all. Either way, the participants in the meeting are naked (metaphorically speaking). Their inflections, eye movements, body language and other behavioural traits are all exposed. Experts in gesture can train the businessman to understand the vocabulary of the body. But even if you don't know the precise significance of a clenched fist on the thigh, or a tug on the left earlobe, judgment is subconsciously affected by all this "non-verbal communication" (NVC).

"He seemed nervous" actually sums up a very complex set of observations. When the party of the second part is well known, the expert manager gets to recognise the NVC which sets alarm-bells ringing, or conversely gives the signal to lie back in the swivel chair, light a large cigar and relax. You can pick up the same kind of message from tone of voice, but the telephone can't provide the confirmation of, say, the shadow that passes over a basically honest man's eyes when he is about to tell a lie. If that slightly suggests the style of an interrogation, it should: that element certainly exists – and some managers have turned it into a whole corporate culture.

Harold S. Geneen, builder of the once-famed ITT conglomerate, not only travelled the Atlantic regularly to inspect his underlings, but reduced some of them to quivering wrecks by the withering inquisitions staged before their peers (that trick being made somewhat easier in Europe by his insistence on sticking to American time). In the electronic era as in earlier days, in one form or another, the role of the boss must include making his stewards give an account of their stewardship. The written reports, the bar-charts, the graphs and the accounts give the essential materials for the process, but it's the personal questioning, the application of pressure, the to-and-fro of debate which finally give both parties the understanding of what's going on.

But it's this very process that the office revolution is changing permanently. First, the boss no longer needs to ask the questions, because he already has the answers – in his work station. Second, and by the same token, he doesn't have to travel the world to exercise control. Third, the Geneen concept of control is a casualty of the revolution, and not before time. The technology now enables the chief executive to be involved and informed as policy develops and as decisions either pay off or misfire – and misfiring, anyway, should become less common as interaction becomes more and more the dominant management mode.

This won't dispense with the need for contact in the superior-subordinate relationship. The distant general who stays aloof from the troops is as common in civilian life as in war, but is rarely the great leader. Part of the latter's genius lies in the ability to communicate through physical presence; business life has many examples to match those of Bernard Montgomery turning round the Eighth Army, or Matthew B. Ridgeway revitalising the UN forces in Korea. You only had to hear Sir John Harvey-Jones address an audience to understand why this longish-haired extrovert with the naval touch and the way with words carried a whole giant company along with his revolution at ICI: face-to-face verbal contact was a formidable weapon in his armoury.

There are other business leaders who use the telephone as a cavalryman did his sabre. It is awe-inspiring, in a way, to behold the change in attitude, from command to cringe, of a powerful subordinate suddenly interrupted by his master's phoned voice. But such regimes are no more likely than Geneen's periodic interrogations to produce the collaborative, dynamic corporate culture from which the greatest and most lasting business success generally flows. The cultured effect works deep down the company: workforces, like electorates, prefer to see the people for whom they work or vote. The briefest eye contact is immeasurably more powerful than the company magazine.

But is all that contact truly obsolescent? Will the few telecommuters of today be the majority of tomorrow? To get Rank Xerox's wonderful savings (eating deep, remember, into the two-and-a-half times salary required to employ a worker in central London), you must have (as Francis Kinsman pointed out) a management with diamond-hard corporate objectives, superb communication, excellent team-building, the hard-to-get combination of formality and flexibility, and a very clear-headed appreciation of which individuals can telecommute and which can't.

Achieving that intimidating standard, however, is simply becoming easier. The new technology forces managements to make up their minds about objectives; through the operations of the network, to decide on aims is automatically to communicate them; the network is founded on the principle of team-working; by creating a shared formal framework, the system allows far more flexibility; and experience using the in-house network will prove effective in creating more potential telecommuters. But none of this will remove one crucial element of contact.

The high probability is that people will need a regular laying on of hands and eyes to prevent dissociation – or to accent the feeling of association. In the pre-electronic era I was myself out on a limb in New York, limited to terse cable contact with the London office of the *Financial Times* and often only persuaded by the appearance of my stories (and my pay) that the paper still knew of my existence. Although in some awe of my editor, I would have (almost) welcomed a personal visit. There is also the possibility that, being an acute psychologist, he would have added to his useful store of knowledge about me.

This personal databank is one that can only be assembled by direct contact. One chairman took over a project for his managing director while the latter was on holiday. He talked to the executive in charge, and, after being assured that all was well, relayed the comforting message over the phone to his holidaying colleague. "Did he say that?" demanded the aghast man. "I'm coming back at once."

That could only arise in the pre-revolutionary company where executives don't know each other's business because they have no method of finding out, except (as in that case) by accident. In a revolutionised company, the computer, rather than the holidaying executive's head, would have possessed a firm grasp of the project, and the chairman could have picked up the reins with far more certainty. But in the end, there is no substitute for the workings of the amazing computer in the skull – and, no less than the emotional human being it directs, it requires all the input of all the senses to satisfy its needs and come to its conclusions.

Not only will the airline executives go on counting their business-class chickens for a long time yet, but so can the builders and lessors of offices. The very fact that the office is dispensable, though, will change its lifestyle. Presence in the office will not be synonymous with the performance of duties. Contribution will matter more than conscientious keeping or exceeding of office hours. The numbers will be smaller, the contacts more frequent and the back-up staff less in evidence. IT will have taken over the structured activities, applying systems analysis and providing systems to help improve *efficiency* – doing things right. But, to use Peter Drucker's brilliant distinction between the two, the next stage will improve *effectiveness* – doing the right things.

By enabling management to improve its understanding, the new technology can at last provide the support for unstructured activities –

developing a strategy, analysing problems, planning and communicating initiatives, etc – that has so far been lacking. This office structure will be the very contradiction of the cork-lined room which keeps out the world; that is the condition to which many executive offices did degenerate as cumbersome systems and layers of hierarchy pushed people into their expensive cells and kept them imprisoned. The technological revolution opens out the office and gives people the chance to be free – and not only the telecommuters.

BOOK II
The Shock of the New

Chapter 6

THE KEY OF INFORMATION

"Merely a tool for storing and transmitting information." That, according to an introduction in the *McKinsey Quarterly*, is how many managers regarded the computer in the summer of 1987. But as the article being introduced pointed out, strange things happen when computers become a "shared technology". The author, Sara Kiesler, is a professor of social sciences and social psychology working at the Robotics Institute at Carnegie-Mellon University in Pittsburgh. And she concludes that sharing computers "influences not only the organisation of work, but also the work itself and enters the domain of management".

By the summer of 1989, the number of managers aware of this incontrovertible fact was certainly far greater than two years previously. It was still a minority, possibly not even a large one. By the summer of 1999, however, nearly all managers will have faced up to, or been faced by, the "many questions about the impact of computers on the workplace" which Kiesler found being asked in 1986:

1. Does a computer network make managers more effective?
2. When introducing computer mail in an organisation, do managers spend less time in decision-making?
3. What kind of computer conference system is best suited to long-distance management?
4. What are the changes technologies make that people care about the most?

Writing only three years later, these questions seem interesting, but not especially relevant. Computer networks will be as commonplace as telephone switchboards by 1999, and no sentient management will install networks without facilities for electronic mail or conferencing. Therefore, the argument over benefits and technological changes will fall into disuse, along with the manual typewriter and the duplicator.

51

Once superior technologies are available, they sweep all (including doubters and opponents) before them.

Kiesler has an interesting analogy with the elevator. No elevators, she points out, no skyscrapers. Originally, people were terrified of the things. Then they and their use became commonplace. The elevator technology "made it possible to build structures that increased the number of people who lived and worked in proximity but did not know each other".

The result was thus to create the office of the past: full of people who "live and work surrounded by strangers" and who "feel more alienated and distanced from each other than they did before the advent of the skyscraper". The office revolution is precisely the opposite of this alienation, this distancing. The new technology brings together those whom the office block drives apart – completing the process which began with the telephone.

As Kiesler points out, when Alexander Graham Bell's great invention became accepted (after the usual process of rejection and delay), "many managers imagined they would use the telephone to enhance their control; they thought that when they were physically absent, they could use the telephone as a broadcast device for transmitting orders and information to the employees." The telephone's powers of two-way communication, however, proved decisive. "It gave employees a chance to talk back to the supervisors, to exchange information, and to send it up the hierarchy as well as receive it."

In the consequent "democratised" workplace, however, the hierarchical order was preserved in large part by the possession of information. The phone could be used for transmitting information – but the data could not be stored in the telephone system, nor accessed save through the voice of a phone user. The only exceptions were two inventions made long after Bell – the recorded message and its variant, the answering machine.

In hindsight, these humdrum and readily accepted tools presage the network revolution. The recorded message turned the telephone into an information tool, with the disadvantages that the disembodied voice giving train times or other information couldn't be interrogated; that the message couldn't be searched for relevant facts, but had to be run through in sequence; and that the message couldn't be updated with ease, save in entirety. Still, the recorded message made its limited information available without paper or human intermediary. It was a beginning.

The answering machine shares the above disadvantages, but made possible the next great advance: a dialogue, of sorts, and above all, storage. It also operates in time and space: that is, events (the incoming messages) are recorded and stored as they occur and can be tapped into at the convenience of the operator wherever he or she may be – thanks to the device of remote access. Thus, the telephone system's familiar features give a foretaste of what, with far greater versatility and power, the networked computer will make just as familiar in the years ahead.

Kiesler, in fact, picks out the impact of computers on communications as the "critical new area for managers to understand and exploit". That, however, implies a degree of control which may be absent. She talks about people overcoming "temporal and geographical barriers" to exchange information; about "computer-mediated communications" being able to "break down hierarchical and departmental barriers, standard operating procedures and organisational norms". If she is right – and it's very hard to argue persuasively against the case – senior managers don't face a need to "understand and exploit" the IT explosion, but must seek to gain some degree of control over a runaway engine.

The potentially vulnerable "barriers" which Kiesler mentions form the cement that binds together all existing organisations. Thus, two enormous problems loom. First, how does management manage the effects of the office revolution on the organisation? Second, what kind of organisation can replace the shattered norms without any loss of efficiency or effectiveness? Actually, the second problem is more intense still. For the overriding purpose of the investment in new technology is to become *more* efficient and effective, not to mark time, still less to move backwards.

Electronic mail provides Kiesler with an excellent illustration of her case. In itself, it appears mostly to substitute for letters, memos, etc., but also, to some extent, for phone calls, conferences and face-to-face meetings. None of these substitutes, however, seems to have the potential to change organisations, any more than the digital watch, in replacing or substituting for clockwork, altered the nature of either time or its telling. But Kiesler points to three features of electronic mail that do have organisational consequences: no intermediary between sender and recipient, no "hard" copy, any format the sender likes.

She sees two hidden effects. The computer can't convey "dynamic personal information": that is, you don't know how the message has been received, and recipients don't know how you feel about the message. Second, a computerised message conveys no personal information about its sender: no letterhead, no signature, no job title. Both of these effects sound a trifle sinister; but depersonalising communication actually and paradoxically seems to Kiesler to be a virtue: "When social definitions are weak or non-existent, communication

53

becomes unregulated. People are less bound by convention, less influenced by status, and unconcerned with making a good appearance. Their behaviour becomes more extreme, impulsive and self-centred. They become in a sense freer people."

The contribution of electronic mail to loosening up communications may well seem exaggerated by this argument. But reduce the discussion to cases, and practical and potentially valuable consequences do appear. Kiesler cites:

1. A large and experienced electronic mail user whose administrators got some twenty-three messages daily; about 60% of these messages (which mostly arose from distribution lists) would not have been received in any other way.
2. In the same company, distribution lists locking together groups who share interests in the same non-business activities and subjects.
3. In another firm, "a product developer's message asking for suggestions about how to add a feature to a product was sent to distribution lists that reached hundreds of people. Within two weeks, he had received more than 150 messages cutting across geographical, departmental, divisional and hierarchical boundaries. Some of the messages told the manager quite bluntly why it was a bad idea to add the feature."

Frankly, the examples make electronic mail sound like a computerised Tower of Babel. Sending administrators twenty-three messages a day, whether they like, want or read them or not, seems like an aggravation of the worst excesses of the paper-driven bureaucracy. Linking colleagues who share an interest in Chinese cooking and science fiction doesn't sound like a wonderfully valuable contribution to the wealth of nations or companies, either. And these 150, no doubt conflicting, messages still left the burden of decision firmly on the product developer's shoulders.

Had the message been replied to by fifteen people, or fifteen hundred, the result would have been no different. But imagine a situation where the company is considering an assault on a new user market: the database can immediately select all executives who have experience relevant to that sector and bring them together, so to speak, via the computer, which can also check external databases for relevant information. All this can be done swiftly, without finding new staff, without bringing people together from widely separated locations, and without having to make their movements coincide in time as well as space.

But is the quality of communication affected by the switch from paper to electronics? Kiesler reports one experiment which suggests that "electronic" groups, never meeting face-to-face, are slightly more prone to take risks. As reported, however, the experimental evidence is too scanty to give much support to the idea that, because "computer-mediated communication reduces social context information and increases self-centredness", you get a less inhibited, more outspoken, more participative result.

These developments may occur: but evidently they will not follow any especially useful pattern unless the processes are given a decisive helping hand, or rather shove, from above. The process of management, in other words, has to be deliberately reconstructed to take advantage of, and to accommodate, the social consequences of investment in new technology. By the very nature of the process, its costs can be measured, but its benefits cannot. For the salesman, of course, this is an opportunity of purest gold. Indeed, the history of IT has been spattered with promises of unquantifiable benefits – promises made to seduce the purchaser away from an all too quantifiable cost.

Kiesler quotes an IT executive at Westinghouse Electric who told her that "I can measure how much this video teleconferencing equipment costs and guess about how much it saves us in travel expenses, but I haven't the slightest idea how good the decisions are that our people reach when they use it." He seems to have a point. Freeing salesmen to make more calls (which IT will also do) should equate with more sales, on reasonable assumptions about consistent hit rates. But managers aren't being freed to make *more* decisions. The idea is that the *quality* of decisions should improve, as the decision-maker spends more time in thinking. But this doesn't accord with the view of most writers on decision-making, who stress the desirability of all due haste and note that, while procrastination may shift the odds in favour of success, the gain will not be great.

There's a probable analogy with another mental process, the comprehension of written matter. Go back over every word, and you will double the time taken, but improve comprehension by 3% to 7% – and that's all. There's no Celsius scale against which to measure the quality of decisions or any other aspect of management. However, no scale is needed – and this time for a good reason that has nothing to do with salesmanship.

All the functions currently being performed inside offices and by managers require various pieces of equipment. All of these either are or will be driven by sophisticated electronics. Each change will enhance the functions of the equipment to an immediately obvious degree. Nobody bothers to count the cost-benefit of switching to a word processor from a manual typewriter or changing over to a digital telephone exchange – any more than managers do sums to justify the purchase of a mobile telephone. The gains in convenience and effectiveness are there, and they will be taken, without the cost per transaction being counted.

The computer fits into this context, and on to the manager's desk, because its screen can bring together all the streams of information that currently reach that same desk. Again, the functionality is visibly, undeniably and most valuably enhanced. You can find what you want to know, and do so immediately. It is an offer you cannot refuse, and ultimately all executives will have to accept it – as they long ago accepted the pocket calculator: before its advent, very few senior managers would have used an adding machine, any more than they managed their own filing cabinets.

Once the computer, the electronic super-filing cabinet, is on that desk, the major cost has been sunk. The other facilities – networking itself, electronic mail, spreadsheets, desk diaries and so on – are inexpensive additions that enormously enhance the utility of what is already highly enhanced equipment. The issue of cost-effectiveness doesn't have to be faced objectively – and can't be, anyway. How do you value the competitive advantage which Japanese companies evidently gain from their assiduous and intensive gathering of information about products, services, technology, their competition, distribution systems, other national economies, and so on?

The positive value of information can only be established by a negative. Failing to keep abreast of rapidly changing technology in products and processes is an obvious, excessive and potentially lethal cost: the equivalent of the "cost of non-conformance" which is the hidden burden bending the backs of companies without modern quality management. Information technology holds the key that unlocks access to the answers which all organisations need, but which many cannot find: in innumerable cases, because they don't even know where to look.

The argument that IT can create competitive advantage has been repeated so often that, like the concept of competitive advantage itself, it runs the risk of becoming yesterday's cliché. But it happens to be tomorrow's truth. In the nineties, companies will have to create information systems that support and help to achieve dynamic expansion for their businesses. The alternative has all too many precedents: failed companies whose managers at all levels didn't know what they were doing. Against this reality, the price of Office Systems Technology is not the critical issue. As so often in management (even in decision-making), the apparently subjective measure tells the truth. It (or IT) must be well worth the cost.

Chapter 7

THE INFORMATION OVERLOAD

Information systems only fully justify their cost when they provide strategic value. There is a crucial difference between benefiting fully from intelligence – by converting it into understanding – and merely receiving information. The alleged information overload of the modern executive is commonly said to have lessened understanding through its sheer indigestible mass. Whether or not that is true, the perceived problem of information overload has only been aggravated by the large gap between mere receipt of information and its presentation in a manner which makes it easily understood and readily used.

The perception of overload results from the fact that technology's amazing success in improving the availability of information has left it appearing even more intractable and hard to construe. And it's true that the advent of systems – departmental or corporate – has given managements the opportunity to access an amount of data too vast to be ingested, let alone digested. In addition to internal systems, those outside the company (such as value-added databases) are contributing by the day, hour and minute to the flood of data, and the flow will never cease. The torrent of professional information generated within the firm, or directly impinging on it from outside, has gathered an unstoppable momentum.

The spate would have swollen in any event, in line with the mounting scale, complexity and diversity of all business and every organisation. The computer, in major part an essential response to this complication, can't avoid also intensifying the problem by spewing more and more data into the flood. Although the typical manager has shunned the keyboard and the screen even more than the printed page (which he is typically too "busy" to read), it's impossible to shun an electronic output which to many seems like an electronic threat.

Yet there was a time when the threat seemed like a dream of the office paradise. In the sixties there was much talk of MIS – "management information systems" – that would be "total". All the facts and figures needed to manage the corporation, be it never so big, would be fed into gigantic number-crunchers. These systems were supposed to remove middle managers by the million. The skyscrapers would empty as the routine tasks were taken over by the mighty electronic brain at the centre. The mindless mammoth would automatically provide the information on which the human giants in their small, secluded executive suite would base their few necessary and (so it was hoped) brilliant decisions.

Once the decisions had been taken, all the sub-decisions would automatically flow, with the results monitored night and day, not by office-bound humans, but by computer sensors indifferent to their habitat. Technically, the dream or nightmare is perfectly feasible. Already, unsleeping computers behave in much the same way as those visions foresaw. All over the world reports are automatically checked. Adjustments can be made instantly to the news of a 13.278% fall in sales in Des Moines, Iowa, a mechanical breakdown in Glenrothes, Scotland, the latest shift in the exchange rate of the dollar against the pound.

But the instability of exchange rates points to the crucial failure in the concept of the total MIS. It was predicted on a steady state – on a largely predictable business universe. That never really existed. But the last two decades have seen such mounting and unpredictable instability that even the world's most powerful computers (in fact, much faster and more powerful than the dream or nightmare machines, and growing in speed and power with every passing year) could never cope with the resulting corporate complexities.

Computers are too rational: the current models (though not the future miracles already on the electronic drawing board) do only what they have been told. Human brains, being more flexible, are better able to make up their own rules as they go along. Notoriously, that's how the latest, crucial turn in the computer saga was born. Middle managers in America, having survived their threatened species status, began to smuggle the first personal computers into the office to help in their jobs. This popular movement reached such proportions that mainframe computer makers were forced late into the market with products that now sell in months what the manufacturers concerned thought might be achieved over years – a prize example in itself of the surprise-full economy in which all businesses now operate.

This consumer-led revolution provides the context in which the old MIS has resurfaced, only in quite different form. It now hinges, not around number-crunching colossi costing tens of millions, but around little boxes which in 1989 rarely cost as much as £10,000, and will very certainly continue to become much cheaper. Today the magic letters are not MIS, but EIS – "executive information systems". Managers can link PCs with the corporate database; in the privacy of their own computers, they can call up all the company information they want (or are allowed) and manipulate the facts and the figures as required.

Nor is this another futuristic dream. Several suppliers offer as staple products systems which provide full-colour presentation of all the information which the executive wants – at the touch of a button. Many such systems are now in use, mostly with large corporations. Without question, however, companies of any size will be able to achieve exactly the same result: their information systems, too, will be able to supply what the executive needs at modest cost, but most immodest speed.

The vital words, though, are "what the executive needs". They hold the answer to the apparent danger that, with this full-spate flood of information available, in all these forms, managers will sink below the waters and disappear without trace – along with the investment in information technology. That would be no mean disappearance. According to McKinsey statistics, thirty-five American banks alone managed to work through $9 billion of spending on computer systems and IT in 1986, and their bills have been getting higher and higher ever since.

If experience to date is anything to go by, moreover, the billions will go on buying massive disappointment. Alan Cane commented in the *Financial Times* that "despite enormous expenditure the banks and financial institutions have no guarantee that they will secure lasting commercial advantage from their investment." In other words, the managements feel they must spend the money: their problem is how. But the special difficulties of such vast operations, which live (or die) on processing and reacting to myriads of small pieces of information (Citibank wants a system to process 170 million instructions *a second*) shouldn't intimidate other managers.

They should follow the example of the head of the enormous Japanese electric utility – or rather his information suppliers. They told the chief executive that he could have a dozen pieces of information always at his fingertips. He only had to name the items. He swiftly came up with variables like the price of oil, the dollar-yen rate, the status of his power stations and the weather forecast, which were all obviously crucial in his business. The IT experts gave him all dozen, told him how to manipulate the data to obtain read-outs on the effects of changes, and promised to return at once if any of the dozen, in *his* view, needed to be replaced.

In other words, the driving force of the system was the driver, which is how it should be. To use another metaphor, the way out of the information maze is to establish where you want to go. Managers are by no means alone in having to cope with huge overloads of information. That's the permanent condition of the human brain. It is very efficient, however, at screening out the useless data from the incessant bombardment of stimuli and only concentrating on the information and observations it needs – often in a highly selective fashion.

Take the new car phenomenon. Buy some dream machine that you think to be a choice rarity, and the roads will suddenly seem full of the cars – you have programmed yourself to notice them. By much the same token, the effective manager programmes his information system to tell him what he wants to know. The "overload" illusion is created mostly by what may be called "passive" data: that is, you are looking at a sheet, or several sheets, or whole volumes of data that stare back meaninglessly from the paper.

Meaning is unlocked by activating information through seeking the answers to questions. For instance, take competition. Managers who by the end of the eighties hadn't gathered that success or failure in competition would govern their fates into the foreseeable, and very probably the unforeseeable future, should have been as rare as the white buffalo – and faced the certain prospect of becoming just as extinct. To meet future competition, the competitor must know where he stands competitively in the here and now.

So the would-be competitor must ask questions like: What are my sales as a proportion of those of my three largest competitors? How has that ratio changed over the past year? That leads on to the much more important question: How can I increase this vital statistic this year – and next? To answer that poser, it helps greatly to know (not think, *know*) what customers think of you and your products and your services in relation to the competition. That, too, can be discovered factually: but only if the company is prepared to expend the time, trouble and money to find out.

All such information fits into the category that Andrew Lloyd Webber might call Really Useful Information. If a manager is drowning in truly useless information, it's either his fault or the company's. All businesses generate huge quantities of information, but most managements are quite inept at mining this cheap internal treasure, let alone the gold (inevitably more expensive) which can be obtained from outside. Board meetings or other managerial discussions often grind to an agonising halt because nobody present has the facts without which matters cannot proceed.

In the board or meeting rooms of the future (and in some progressive companies, those of the present), this full stop will rarely occur, because the screens (full size if need be) will swiftly summon up the missing matter. All that's needed is the readiness of managers to accept that information has become an office resource which is on tap, just like the telephone. But that requires the same education, or the same pressure of necessity, that has already turned executives in the City of London and on Wall Street into dedicated screen-watchers.

Managers used to have the excuse that personal computers were "ornery and hard to use", in the words of *Business Week*. But the mouse technology developed by Xerox Corporation at its Palo Alto Research Corporation has led the way into a new generation of easy-to-use machines which are hardly ever "ornery": as ease of use increases and prices decrease, the onward march of the PC will be impossible for the most conservative of managers to resist. But this kind of information – the controllable, the mandatory, the requested, the stored – is only part of the picture.

It's the random news, views and ideas picked up from wide reading that may make all the difference between a business nothing and a corporate something, even between millions and billions. It is, of course, true that any manager who tried to read everything of any conceivable value would rapidly run out of time in which actually to manage. But that's no excuse for not reading at all. The solution is the same as that for coping with masses of internal data. There you must decide what you need to know, what questions you want to ask, and to have answered; with outside information sources, you must select what you will always read, while leaving some time for the random reading that may well prove the most valuable – *if you know what you're looking for.*

The italicised words hold the clue to the failure of middle managers to disappear. Complexity means that the number of options has multiplied. A traffic light is an automaton, which runs through a strictly regulated process of red, amber and green. The positioning of the light is also a relatively simple decision: yes or no to its installation at this particular junction. But introduce the timing of the light to produce the smoothest traffic flow throughout the day, allow overrides from central control to meet changed circumstances, and the per-mutations and combinations become infinite.

In disentangling the options to arrive at the optimum solution, human choice has to master the process, responding to the best and fastest information available. The same principle applies to the life of the office and the organisation which it, the control room, directs. More and more structured work will be delegated to the automata and the automatic processes; but that devolution is being accompanied by intensified pressure for higher-level decisions from the human beings who (among their other choices) must choose what to automate and how.

Viewed objectively, the information overload does not exist. Rather, there's an information *underload*. Decisions are still being taken every minute on the basis of inadequate information inadequately analysed. The new technology has the capacity to cut through the alleged overload to reach the essential information which it contains. But that capacity won't be utilised unless managements are prepared to exercise the ruthlessness shown by one chief executive whose drive to eliminate useless paper was getting nowhere.

Every form and report, it seemed, was regarded as essential, by someone somewhere in the organisation. So this tough-minded man started killing the documents one by one unannounced, waiting for complaints. Nobody noticed the disappearances until he began to reach the really useful bedrock. In another company, the same technique, after a considerable time-lag, met resistance when people finally noticed the absence of various regular reports. The cunning top manager and paper-cutter resumed the distribution of the missing folders, with one difference: they contained blank paper. Nobody noticed.

The overload is the creation of bad managements which have used the new technology as a bad excuse for their sloppiness. Good management, by tackling its information load as a production resource, can achieve the same brilliant economies and improvements that the Japanese won by the invention of *kanban* – essentially an information system, based with utmost simplicity on coloured cards, for controlling stocks and directing their on-time and just-in-time distribution. The office is essentially an information system for controlling and directing the life and success of the organisation. Viewed and treated in that light, it becomes a different and far more powerful entity.

Chapter 8

THE CHALLENGE OF IT

The thinking of managers about the future of the office, or "the office of the future", has been conditioned by their point of entry into this new world. The very word "future" implied that this was a problem for tomorrow rather than today. The diseconomies of the office of the present, in terms of both costs and managerial under-performance, have been heavy enough to demand urgent action all through the period in which electronics has been making its way through office equipment, piece by piece.

It all began, unfortunately, with the typewriter. "Word processing" was the inspired piece of copywriting used to describe what was basically a typewriter (a system for text entry), to which editing, word storage and document retrieval had been added. The advantages of these additions are obvious and immediate, just like those of computerising the payroll. Like the mainframe computer before it, the word processor remained a clerical substitute, nothing to do with management, independent of all other equipment in the office, and having little or no effect on how anybody worked – except to reduce typist error and effort.

Getting an improved model, even greatly improved, is not the same as acquiring an entirely new technology. But entry via the typewriter meant that the personal computer, in its turn, tended to be seen as an advanced word processor, with the huge advantage that it could perform many other tasks: the advantage was redundant in most cases, since the PC (again repeating experience with larger computers) has been used overwhelmingly as a glorified typewriter with a built-in filing system.

Studies show that 80% of the use of PCs is as word processors. Users of IBM-compatible machines on average, as noted in Chapter 2, employ only four of the multitudes of programs available, and one of those, without question, will be for word processing. Most of the time, the machines have stood idle, dumb, despite their amazing capacity for industriousness and reactive intelligence. Other office functions have been automated alongside, but not around the PCs, which haven't even been integrated with each other.

In the summer of 1989, an executive in one of Britain's largest companies was complaining that, on a visit to headquarters, he found half a dozen different PC systems: nobody could use any of them to make a simple change in a document produced on a PC in his own subsidiary. This company is involved in the highest of technology – in telecommunications. Small wonder that its less sophisticated customers had still to awaken to the virtues of integrating their communications with the rest of their office systems.

They are not, of course, seen as "systems". But the screens are the eyes, ears and tongues of text-processing systems: processing words, retrieving text-based information, storing and accessing documents. Their integration, being built-in, isn't obvious: but it's the computer which automatically "takes" the document from the typist, meta-phorically crosses the office to file the electronic paper in the correct file, from which it will automatically reappear as the invisible filing clerk digs it out. The system has bound together disparate operations into a cohesive whole.

The cohesion has extended to linking text-processing with the data-processing conducted in other systems – which really are systems, installed by experts, often at considerable expense, to manipulate and store the corporate database. That hasn't been repeated in com-munications generally. The explosion of technology has introduced a confusing crowd of new words and concepts into the management vocabulary – local area networks, viewdata, teletext, electronic docu-ment distribution, and electronic mail – but in 1990 few had found their way into regular management use.

Moreover, these are currently voiceless systems, existing side by side with the actuality or coming appearance of vocal transmissions over private multifunction digital telephone exchanges, together with systems for voice recognition, voice response and voice-based messag-ing. And in the same offices, on the same desks, but generally in independence, are the microcomputers, with their capacities for decision support, graphic presentation, spreadsheet work and access to the external data carried on the databases which are being con-structed at dizzying pace all over the world.

Managements which have started to grapple with the questions posed by this formidable array of hardware – and the accompanying variety of software, which is to all intents and purposes infinite – have understandably been advised to concentrate on straightforward questions. Writing in *The Complete Guide to Modern Management*, which I edited in 1988, Michael duQuesnay suggested four:

1. What systems do I introduce now and in the near future?
2. How do I prove or measure the benefits of these expensive systems?
3. How do I handle the implementation of systems which directly and dramatically affect everyone from the directors to the secretaries?
4. Can I afford to buy now and waste a lot of time and resources on unproven or unsuccessful systems?

What was left unsaid, or unasked, could hardly be more fundamental. None of the questions goes to the heart of the matter: *How is this company going to be managed, and how must the office be organised to achieve the management objectives?* Information technology has long presented a challenge to management – a challenge which has wrongly been presented in terms of coping with the complexities and changes of the technology itself. These have, indeed, been amazing, and all the more difficult to handle for being largely unpredicted: very few people in 1970 foresaw distributed processing or the surge of the minicomputer, or the rise of the PC and executive work station.

But the latter phenomenon highlights the true nature of the challenge. As noted earlier, with the initial introduction of the PC, individual managers took the law into their own hands; they far anticipated corporate decisions as they responded to the challenge of running their own increasingly complex jobs inside management structures where, whether top management liked it or not, considerable executive power was moving down the line to operating managers. The new challenge is that top management itself has been drawn willy-nilly into the arena: the issue is not cost, but management itself.

Of course, the economics, as with any business decision, have to be weighed, and here the disappointments have been numerous – even innumerable. Initially, establishing the economic benefits seemed to provide little trouble. The consultants Booz Allen & Hamilton appeared to demonstrate that white-collar workers were spending up to a quarter of their time non-productively. Against that background, their estimate that productivity improvements as high as 15% could be attained through improved technology sounded eminently reasonable.

The earlier experience of the computer age appears to have been repeated: over-optimism on both sides of the equation, costs and productivity, has led to disillusion, to the view that the office of the future is as much a chimera as the Total Management Information System mentioned in Chapter Seven: the huge one-stop system, built around the largest mainframes on the market, that was supposed to subsume the entire corporation. DuQuesnay quotes Paul Strassmann, author of *Computer Pay-off*, to the effect "that recent studies have shown no direct correlation between increased investments in technology and increased management productivity".

Strassmann, who until 1985 was chief information systems executive and vice-president of the information products group of Xerox Corporation, also points out that "in a poorly managed business, increased capital costs serve only to increase the cost of management, so that productivity goes down." The key words are "poorly managed". A well-run firm, seeking answers to the key question italicised above (*How is this company going to be managed, and how must the office be organised to achieve the management objectives?*), will not simply pile on capital costs: it may still be unable to show quantifiable benefits – not if the benefits are like those quoted by a Plessey executive, whose services include electronic mail: "Because of this system I can turn round messages and internal communications four times a day instead of once or twice."

DuQuesnay notes that this "might allow a company to respond consistently to a customer in one day instead of three or four previously". He cites a large firm of City lawyers which believes that the extra speed generated by an automated, integrated office system has attracted overseas customers to put deals together in London. These quoted benefits, moreover, are not end-products of the office revolution. They merely mark the early stages of the progress from capabilities to systems.

Any office with the right to call itself modern started the year 1990 with computing capacity round which seven key capabilities revolved: advanced telephone systems, electronic filing, word processing, microcomputing, electronic document distribution, electronic mail and forms processing. By the end of the decade, these clerical functions will have been largely superseded by executive systems – outnumbering the functions, what's more, by at least two.

The seven functions, which duQuesnay calls "core applications", will be but one of the nine systems he foresees: seven others are management information, conferencing, business graphics, decision support, activity management, personal office aids, and external information retrieval: the eighth is "special applications". As he observes, in the process of this move from capabilities to management, "distinctions between data processing systems, telecommunications systems and text processing systems will become blurred".

This giant leap forward has seemed more like a stumble because suppliers, repeating a marketing error of the mainframe era, oversold integration before they could actually supply or even demonstrate the necessary product line. DuQuesnay reports that in consequence there's been "a change in an area where the introduction of new products has traditionally been supplier-led rather than responding directly to user-requirements and needs".

Customer leadership consists initially of questions like this: Why can't we create documents on a word processor, store them in the mainframe files, and get access to them via a desktop terminal through our brand-new digital phone exchange? After all, the customers may well say, the exchange is supposed to be able to transfer data as well as voice messages. The questions are reasonable, and the customers will get what they want – and more, as the pace of technology continues to escalate.

What they get out of the investment, however, depends on them. Paul Strassmann's efforts to find an appropriate measure for the return on IT investment had a "surprisingly simple result", he has said. "I found that management, not capital, is decisive." Strassmann's concept, the "return on management", measures how much value management adds to a business – "value" being what is left after all direct and indirect costs, and payments to shareholders and suppliers, have been deducted. IT is one component of the costs involved.

The core of the approach, and indeed that of the office revolution, is that marketing and strategy issues are brought into the equation. The objective of investment in new office technology should be to raise the added value contributed by management. As Strassmann argues, it's not enough to suppose that the process is semi-automatic: strategic importance and productivity should be the starting points for decisions: instead they have been "devalued and abused" as information systems managers scurry to justify proposals for massive investment.

"It's the risk level, not the returns, which can be critical," he says. Boards, however, are asked to make their judgments on "pathologically inaccurate" figures: "The fault lies with the profuse use of spreadsheets ... People compensate for risks by making conservative estimates. Those numbers are further polluted when they are multiplied. Boards either have the choice of believing a conservative estimate, or rejecting it."

The irony is that the powers of IT, in which the spreadsheet is an important ingredient, thus pave the way to their own abuse, and to disappointments – as when Bankamerica, trying to switch from batch processing to a centralised securities transaction system in one blow, fell flat on its face. The major obstacle was imposing a centralised system on a decentralised operation whose people resisted the move.

As Strassmann emphasises, "The rule is deal with one variable at a time. Sort out the organisational issues before changing the system."

It would be easy to be discouraged by his emphasis on the risks involved in making mistakes, his disaster stories of companies that have committed gross errors, his dismissal of "ridiculous claims of benefits yielding 1,000% improvements" and the flat assertion that "There is absolutely no correlation between the level of investment in information technology and performance." But these negative statements are offset by the positive aspects of a fundamental change in the nature of the investment.

The emphasis is no longer on displacing costs. That being so, it makes little sense to justify the money spent by referring to some input/output method of evaluation, like return on assets. The nature of the office revolution is so far-reaching that its benefits, if achieved, can only be described in qualitative terms. How do you quantify, for example, the rewards of investment in a major computerisation project that links a travel company's reservation systems for package tours with all its agents nationwide?

There are simple tests: like, how many more holidays must we sell to cover the cost of the new system? But even if that question produces a discouraging answer, the analysis isn't complete. The company must ask, what do we stand to lose by *not* making the investment – is there a threat to our competitive advantage which will be forestalled by the move, and what is the value of pre-emption? The question is similar to the concept of opportunity cost, in which the issue is what alternative investments are being foregone to make the one that you are considering.

Equally, it calls to mind the concept of relative price, in which a decision not to follow a price leader is a decision to cut your own price. It's far easier to quantify the expense you will actually incur by automating the office, and to compare that with current actuals. But the costs of *not* automating are also actual, and they must mount over time. That's no excuse, as Strassmann says, for sloppy figuring, wishful thinking, exaggeration of benefits and under-assessment of risks. But those four horsemen of the IT apocalypse embody precisely the vices that the virtuously planned, electronics-based management will avoid.

The revolutionised office is a tool for rapid provision of accurate data, the organisation of factually founded thought, reasoned evaluation of returns, and in-the-round, thorough projection of potential outcomes. Absence of these is the greatest possible diseconomy, and the basic reason why the office of the present has become an unacceptably high cost centre. The saving grace is that the transition to the office of the future, once problematical and extremely costly, is rapidly becoming both more certain and much cheaper – especially for those who follow Strassmann's injunction to get the management right first. For that is the fundamental purpose, first and last.

Chapter 9

THE ARCHITECTURE OF EFFECTIVENESS

The idea of information as a crucial resource, perhaps the decisive resource, has been difficult for managers to grasp. That's no doubt because, while information technology has always existed, its discrete components have been viewed separately and kept so distinct that even the notion of "IT" wasn't recognised. Information came in the form of libraries, reports, publications, memos, phone calls, accounts, wire services, and so on. But companies didn't see these as elements in a whole – as parts of a system.

That being so, nobody was in charge of the system. There was no chief information officer. Somebody was responsible for telecommunications. There was a librarian. The finance director and the company secretary had their specific duties. Individual managers subscribed for whatever publications they thought necessary. Only with the coming of the computer was the phrase "information technology" born – and even then it referred to the hardware and software of the computer, and by extension to the structured corporate processes that were computerised.

Some of this work wasn't "information" at all – payroll automation, for example (although it could, in fact, have yielded much valuable management information if properly programmed). A vast amount of corporate information, including all the unstructured processes (as well as much of the structured), was not covered by the IT investment. There was still no real system – and there still isn't, in most organisations. That in itself would matter not at all if the result met all the obvious needs for information on which management can take decisive action. But that is palpably not the case.

There are gaps between the elements that make up the company's primitive IT "system". Required information is often either not available or not known (which comes to the same thing). Information which is available is not collated and not shared. IT which is really "ignorance technology" is not a corporate asset, but a managerial liability. That, too, would be less grave if all managements were equally hampered: but the evolution of modern competition has put paid to that possibility.

Japanese competition, above all, has shown that, with or without advanced electronics, better and wider information is a most powerful weapon in world and local markets. The advance of Japan, as noted in Chapter 6, has been based on keeping abreast of the rapidly changing technology in products and processes. Westerners have complained about the ruthless Japanese exploitation of Western inventions – for example, the advance from nowhere in DRAM electronic chips (standing for "dynamic random access memory") to world leadership in this basic building block of microelectronics. The exploitation, however, has generally involved nothing more than acting on readily available information.

The national appetite for information has become rightly legendary – whether it's obtaining technical specifications or arriving in large numbers at motor races to record in detail everything that will or might affect your own plans. Some of the tales may be apocryphal – have Japanese firms planning investment in Europe really gone into such detailed matters as Territorial Army service in Britain and the possible consequent loss of man-hours? Whatever the truth, they have certainly subscribed to the home town newspapers of American rivals, totally absorbed and greatly improved the techniques of statistical quality control (itself a method based on abstracting and interpreting information), and mastered the mechanics of market after market – and so on.

But this assiduous gathering of information implies something else: that a system exists for ensuring that the information is disseminated and used. That system is obviously inseparable from the management principles on which the Japanese company operates. That emphasis on gathering all relevant information, no matter how detailed, on correlating it for distribution to all parties for whom the information is relevant, and on discussing and analysing the information in groups to arrive at the correct conclusion – all that has no dependence on "technology", new or old.

But true modern information technology, which means the co-ordination and distribution of relevant information flows by the use of electronic hardware and software, rests on precisely the same intellectual framework. The contribution to Western firms made by electronics is to help them bridge in one span the gap between the receipt of information and the evidently more powerful application achieved by many Japanese competitors. Workstations that can communicate with each other and which are linked to the same external and internal databases are an equivalent of the collaborative, data-based management that Japan has developed so intensively.

Managers are reluctant to bridge that span partly because of their accumulated resistance, noted above, to the whole idea of information as a "system"; partly because of fear of the very technology that can actually make computer-phobia a thing of the past; and partly, it has to be said, because management by prejudice is far more common than management by exception, by objectives or by anything else. Listen to any management conversation, and the number of untested propositions put forward as verified facts is astounding; even more astonishing is the fact that verification, as likely as not, will never be attempted.

The winning proposition carries all before it, including the unfilled need to test its own validity. The data processing industry itself is a monument – or rather scores of monuments – to its own unscientific management of information. Lack of knowledge about or evaluation of their customers' needs, and ignoring the technological possibilities for meeting the latter, left all the mainframe makers lagging far behind the pace of the office revolution – and this is only one instance of the sins of omission and commission that perfect, or simply better information would have avoided.

The mainframe makers were wedded to business and to some extent office systems. The conflict, which has been well put by Rank Xerox, is that of office systems versus information systems. Emphasis on the latter rather than the former explains the failure of organisations to gain the full value of their investment in information technology as it has spread through the organisation.

As the company (like this book) stresses again and again, "information is only of strategic value when it results in better understanding." The application of IT to the structured activities (order processing, purchasing, accounting, paying, stocking, calculating) thus has no strategic value. But, as Rank Xerox argues, the technology "has fuelled growth in unstructured activity roles within most organisations" – the roles being strategy, planning, analysis, communication, publishing, changing, researching, and developing: the whole gamut of activities that are generally lumped together as "management".

The task is therefore clear: to use the technology to support the unstructured activities and to bind together unstructured and structured. The barrier lies in the fact that, although the role, capability and justification of IT systems have changed enormously in twenty years, the architecture of data processing has stayed resolutely wedded to the support of transaction processing capability. That replaced computational capability as the core of IT in the 1960s and 1970s, justified by cost savings that, despite all the groans from users, were often gigantic. But over the later 1970s and into the 1980s, database management and networks have become the dominant capabilities – and they demand an architecture that lends itself "to the support of unstructured activities or thinking roles within an organisation".

For the organisation itself has changed: the moves from stable to dynamic environments, and from limited information to a dramatically increased flood of data, have been accompanied by "the growth of thinking roles associated with management professionals, information workers or knowledge workers" – people who may now account (if US studies are any guide) not for a minority of the workforce, but for an overwhelming majority of 70%.

How do these people work? For a start, their workflow is not predictable and what happens within it is heavily conditioned by the vagaries of human behaviour. In their activities, knowledge workers assimilate information from a variety of sources, take (supposedly) informed views or opinions, and communicate the views to others both inside and outside the organisation. In the new office, this information will flow in from internal and external sources predominantly through PCs and other terminals through the workstation. In itself, however, the data is meaningless. It must be related to "the status of thinking and understanding" associated with the subject-matter contained in documents like strategy papers, marketing plans, R & D reports and quality reports.

All this, moreover, takes place in an environment which is subject to interruptions and restarts, and which involves the interchange, exchange and correction of views, knowledge and assumptions. In a replay of the poor linkage between structured and unstructured activities, the technology-assisted inflow of information is poorly connected with the increasingly complex subject-matter to which it is vital. As Rank Xerox puts it, "The task is to capture the relationship between information, views, opinions, experience and draw conclusions, thereby facilitating understanding."

The task, put another way, is to advance from office automation (which "has applied technology to the automation of discrete activities") to office *systems* (in which technology is applied to "the support of overall processes"). That demands a technology "adaptable to any change in the process by which we work and manage: responsive to the unstructured nature of office and managerial roles". The system takes in information from information systems, then allows the end-user "to work with thoughts and conclusions through document management-based architecture, and a human interface, to support the iterative way in which we develop understanding".

Iteration is the act of repetition, and is a word that itself figures repeatedly in discussions of what happens inside the knowledge-based office and the knowledge worker's mind. The analogy is with the scientist, endlessly repeating experiments until the hypothesis has been established and confirmed. The development is from a single observation converted into a single conclusion to many observations combined to achieve a conclusion that has many facets. Rank Xerox defines a document as "a vehicle to facilitate understanding" – as the means by which information passes into understanding and then into communication.

The new electronic office architecture supplies information through access to relevant data and documents. The access is supplied via document management, data management and network services. Understanding requires support in order to be assimilated – and that was the thinking behind the Palo Alto Research Center's creation of "the working desk view", in which the computer display mimics the shape and appearance of the executive's desktop and its normal contents. Finally, fully effective communication demands presentation and creation of "compound documents" – ones that allow any form of illustration so as to fulfil their vehicular role.

It sounds abstract, and is indeed an abstraction from the observed processes of the working office. Only examples can show the practical, concrete impact of information and misinformation. For instance, a market leader in Europe in consumer goods faced a challenge from a new product of equal quality but lower price. The leader decided to combat the launch with a simultaneous, large trade promotion.

So far, so good. But as McKinsey consultants John L. Cecil and Eugene A. Hall reported in the *Harvard Business Review*, "scanner data on actual prices paid were not available" from electronic point of sale equipment. So the challenger didn't know for sure whether retailers were giving customers the full benefit of the leader's allowance – "an uncertainty that sparked internal debate" in the challenging company about whether its own proposed consumer promotion coupon had to match the allowance in full. While the product eventually succeeded, the missing information cost the company an estimated $25 million in revenues.

Note the words "internal debate". Discussions and arguments can't reach enlightened conclusions in the dark. The mistake still made by most managers as the 1990s began, though, was to consider any or all of their missing pieces of information as singular, as the causes of uncertainty and error in themselves. In fact, they are symptoms of a general, truly systemic disease – the failure to move into the new world of information systems.

It will never, of course, be a world of perfect knowledge, perfect communications and perfect decisions. But it will be far in advance of the thinking and the capacities of one multi-national, with a highly capable chairman, managing director and finance director. In mid-1989, the chairman had not yet heard of PC-based executive information systems; of the trio, only one had ever sat in front of a PC – for four abortive hours of training, four years before; and all three were still deterred, remarkably enough, by the least important item in the technology of revolution – the keyboard.

At that date, they were among a great majority. It's as if most senior managers refused to use the telephone because they were unsure of its benefits and frightened of dialling. At the end of the decade, though, the minority will have become the majority. The necessity of making Office Systems Technology effective will be understood, along with the means to that end: that being an architecture, designed to support the true office environment, that allows the full interaction of both office systems and data processing.

The unstructured activities which dominated the lives of that computerless senior executive trio can be thought of as a triangle. Working upwards from the base, you must first acquire information and ensure that you really are gaining access to what is relevant. The next consideration is that knowledge is only achieved by full understanding of the information, which on its own is of little value: so you must understand and relate to it. The object is to improve people's ability to assimilate and understand information readily. With that done, the final step is to communicate that understanding. And, if all that means being able to handle a keyboard, many much tougher challenges will face top managers in an office environment that is changing more fundamentally than not only they, but their employees and many experts believe.

Chapter 10

THE IMPACT OF DOCUMENTATION

The Satex Group, which sponsored the Henley Centre's report on *The Office of the Future*, published in 1989, had the year before commissioned research which showed, unsurprisingly, that "many British companies waste thousands of pounds a year ... by ignoring the costs incurred by inefficient management, untrained buyers, wasted staff time and unnecessary storage space and distribution costs". Its particular concern, that being its business, was stationery and office supplies, and it launched the TMS plan to help control them – TMS standing for saving Time, Money and Space.

In the new office, electronics will automatically manage all three, producing vast improvements as so-called "hard" copy (i.e. soft pieces of paper) gives way to "soft" (i.e. hard storage of electronic impulses). In the Henley report, curiously enough, "technology" occupies only three short paragraphs: including a graph, they account for three-quarters of a page in thirteen pages of text. As for the graph, headed "Office Technology", it merely shows the proportion of companies with a mainframe computer, as assessed by a leading firm of estate agents, Debenham, Tewson and Chinnocks.

While the figures are interesting as far as they go, showing a 70% mainframe penetration in the City of London and the south-east, against a national figure of less than half, they do not, of course, say anything about how far office technology has gone, still less where it is going. The key to the office revolution is the microcomputer and its intelligent housing, the executive workstation. True, the report does mention the "post big-bang dealing desk" installed by the financial houses, which "presented a difficult challenge to the office designer and represents some of the possible innovations for the office of the future": and these desks are executive workstations, of a kind.

That kind, however, is strictly limited in function and purpose. It is closer to clerical automation than to executive work, because the activity of dealers (taking orders and enquiries over the phone, checking prices on the screens, buying and selling over the phone, entering the transactions into the system) are in many ways highly structured. The "challenge" to the office designer, as reported in the very first chapter of this book, has been met by imitating the most structured environment of all: that of the clerking rooms in the big insurance companies before the computer came to the rescue of their worker ants.

Henley's description of the result is perfectly apt. "The space generally allocated to the individual worker in the dealing room is much less than in the conventional office." The designers may seek to provide "maximum user comfort coupled with maximum availability of information input", but the latter, in the shape of accommodation for the "monitors and other hardware needed for modern financial dealings", gets the thick end of the coupling every time. In the true executive floors, symbolically placed above the dealing rooms, designers are not, in the delicate Henley phrasing, "likely to be increasingly called upon to balance functionality, flexibility and comfort economically in terms of cost and floorspace".

As to what will happen in the office proper, Henley notes the "important impact" of technology on functioning, but mentions only two devices: the facsimile machine and the desktop publishing system. Both, it so happens, use paper, although the use is only incremental to the extent that fax replaces phone and that desktop publishing is used where no publishing would have been commissioned before. The report seems to take some comfort in the fact that "The paperless office has not happened yet – indeed innovations such as the fax machine have found new uses for paper communication."

The language is radical in places: "New inventions, such as the fax machine (figures from Roltech show that penetration of fax machines could reach 1m in the UK by 1992), have *revolutionised* [my italics] business communications systems." The take-up of desktop publishing over the past few years, too, has been "*dramatic*" – but it serves as "a good example of why increasing use of electronic systems do [*sic*] not necessarily spell the end of paper-based systems".

Henley accepts that electronic-based systems will gain ground against paper, but thinks that, because "communication and information storage as a whole will increase ... the absolute demand for paper-based systems will continue and possibly even increase further". If the total market doubles over time, in other words, and the proportionate use of paper halves, the amount of paper consumed will stay the same. The writers make the minimal concession to a less well-papered view of the future: "Hard copy will always be required, but perhaps in the longer term, will be needed less often than at present."

This passage was written well into an era when a bank can store several years' records, with swift access to every piece of information they contain, in an electronic storage space measuring a few cubic feet. The references to facsimile were written without reference to the obsolescence, at least for major users, threatened by the rise of electronic mail. Nobody questions that paper will always play an important role, inside and outside the office: after all, this book is printed on paper – and the electronic age has seen an unexpected and unprecedented explosion of demand for both books and periodicals.

In 1988, according to the Book Industry Study Group, hardcover books sold 286 million copies in the United States, a rise of a third over 1983. But most of those paper products were involved, one way or another, in the paperless revolution. This book was written on a personal computer: the manuscript was printed out on paper, but could more easily have been left on disc – saving the publishers the expense of having it set electronically all over again. Technically, no paper was required (not even for the design of the dust-jacket) between the first touch on my keyboard and the printing of the first page.

Nor is any state-of-the-art technology needed to achieve this bonfire of paper. The hardware and the software are routine, used daily in hundreds of thousands of locations as everyday tools. The technology already exists – in practical, demonstrable form – to eliminate virtually every use of paper in every office. In most cases, moreover, significant savings would be made in time and cost (as in the elimination of my paper manuscript in the movement of this text via the editor to the printer) by using conventional equipment which is already installed and paid for.

What is conventional today, however, was revolutionary yesterday. To get some idea of what the future presently holds, and which the Henley Centre did not take into account, consider a report published in *Business Week* on 8th May, 1989:

Last month, a computer at Hughes Aircraft Co in Los Angeles zapped a short memo to a computer nearly 2,000 miles away at Boeing Co – and the age of electronic mail dawned. It wasn't just that the memo took mere seconds to arrive. More impressive was that it crossed previously impenetrable boundaries. With the press of a button, the message left a Hughes IBM computer, was picked up by MCI Mail, transferred to Telemail, then deposited in a Digital Equipment computer at Boeing.

That doesn't sound too miraculous, but the magazine writer was plainly right in saying that "It was a remarkable achievement, even if it did go largely unnoticed." To quote a Hughes manager, "It took us more than a decade to learn that true electronic mail can work." Electronic mail has actually been operating for some time. John Kavanagh, writing in *Finance* magazine, described it as "a cross between the postal, telephone and telex services, with some on-line computing thrown in. It combines the best of all these services, while eliminating their disadvantages." Among the most conspicuous of the drawbacks of the existing services is cost. According to Kavanagh, studies show that it costs £4 in staff costs to send a business letter 150 words long. At best, the letter will take twenty-four hours to pass through the post office system, which has to incur costs of its own in the process.

An electronic mail man complains, justifiably enough, that "a vast expenditure of resources" is required simply to inform somebody that "I am writing to confirm our meeting on the 29th." That message, moreover, will probably be filed at both ends. Electronic mail thus saves all three of the Satex trinity of time, money and space. Kavanagh writes that "an electronic mail message can be delivered in minutes with no human intervention" at the cost of an ordinary stamp – "and if necessary it can be sent to 500 people for the price of a single message." Unlike the phone, electronic mail doesn't require somebody on the other end of the line; unlike facsimile, it doesn't require additional hardware or paper; unlike telex, it doesn't require extra terminals and lines.

For all that, as Kavanagh kept on reminding his readers, "there is a catch." The importance of the barrier-breaking by Hughes and Boeing is that it overcomes the catch. The importance of that, in turn, is that it opens the floodgates to a great onrush of messages. According to a Coopers & Lybrand expert, by 1992 some 16 billion messages – five times the 1988 figure – will be sent via "E-mail", and 60 billion by 2000. Another expert forecasts a 30% annual rise in E-mail revenues, which already topped $400 million in 1988. It could easily become the dominant form of "written" communication between organisations – and very likely between individuals, in and out of offices.

Kavanagh's catch lay in the fact that, although millions of users have been enjoying the benefits of packaged electronic mail programs for internal use, "The package suppliers are selling purely private systems, usually to a captive audience: companies which probably already use their office automation systems or equipment in some way and see electronic mail as a natural addition for internal correspondence. The public services, however, are starting virtually from scratch with every customer."

As he says, it's been like "trying to sell the first telephone: no one is interested until there is someone else to call." In consequence, in the earlier 1980s, says *Business Week*, Western Union spent some $100 million in a year to promote its E-mail service for the miserable return of $20 million in revenues. Until computer could speak to computer, the catch could not be unlocked. "It's as if we told people you can only call other people who have a black telephone," observed Michael Zisman, head of an electronic mail software company. (His metaphor would have been out of place in Britain where, until quite recently, black telephones were all there was.)

The key to a far richer future lay in the new communications standard adopted in 1984 and known as X-dot 400 (or X.400). Here, as in office automation generally, lack of common standards has severely retarded progress. The reason has always been the same: hope among jostling competitors that a proprietary system would give them competitive advantage, and fear that common systems would destroy it. The result, slower growth and worse service, has harmed all parties. Consequently, opposition to common standards is dying – and with its death the future can be born.

E-mail thus epitomises the processes which will make the paperless office not so much an option as omnipresent reality. There are difficulties and commercial disadvantages to overcome. The public networks, for instance, could not in May 1988 communicate with local area networks (LANs), of which there were some 600,000 linking up large American corporations – and a tenth of these used internal electronic mail. Here again, technology is changing the rules of the game: if the work of the Applications Program Interface Committee succeeds, by the time these words are read, standards enabling LANs to join the general E-mail revolution will be in or nearing operation.

A further drawback is cost. At the time of the *Business Week* article, electronic mail messages were costing about $1 to send, or four times the per page cost proposed by a new facsimile network then being marketed. But the cost will be brought down as the traffic mounts – the bill for 60 billion messages in the year 2000 won't be $60 billion in 1990 currency, or anything like it. And E-mail is simply more attractive in several respects: to quote the magazine, "E-mailers will be able to send notes and perhaps even legal documents just by typing in the name of the person they want to reach."

No print-out, no searching for addresses, no need to leave the work station, instant despatch ... in a world where letters may account for 40% of all express-mail deliveries (a business clearly vulnerable to

E-mail competition), the electronic postal service has immense advantages which will only become stronger as the technological relationships are cemented – notably, when the X.500 directory of all users appears in 1993. It's hard to see what can stop E-mail's advance, other than a rival technology: and none is on the horizon.

The April 1989 breakthrough is a sharp reminder that conservative forecasts like Henley's are in a losing race with fast-moving realities. The move to the paperless office has been retarded less by inherent economic factors than by supplier rivalries, customer conservatism and technological gaps. Now the latter are being closed, the role of paper must diminish relatively, and no doubt absolutely. A sentence in *Business Week*'s account about the adoption of the X.400 standard deserves careful pondering: "The public networks were forced into a compromise by powerful customers who grew tired of waiting for open systems."

That is going to happen wherever unnatural obstacles are preventing natural development. The crucial force that E-mail encapsulates is that the office revolution no longer hinges on expensive, untried equipment that companies don't possess. The pivot is well-tried equipment, much of it very cheap, that companies already own, but which must be under-exploited unless they have software that can effectively manage both documents and data, integrating their access, together with excellent network services.

In addition, the ability to understand information must be improved if a number of electronic documents can be presented simultaneously. The hierarchy of interlinked capacities continues: effective presentation is enhanced by the power of illustration through documents that employ images, graphics and text as well as figures. Managers will be able to browse through and work with "compound" documents, using a variety of text, formulae, graphic images and data, that can in turn be reproduced by office publishing capacity.

Beyond these electronic talents, and just over the technological horizon, lies the use of artificial intelligence to support further the human interaction with the new and powerful office tool called the executive work station. At its simplest level, like the direct input of my electronic manuscript into electronic typesetting equipment, the removal of the paper link will add no costs and save time, money and space in previously unimagined amounts. Further up the hierarchy, it will open the door leading to a new age that is inevitable – and imminent.

BOOK III
The Organisational Upheaval

Chapter 11

THE ORGANISATIONAL IMPERATIVE

By far the most authoritative and compelling vision of the revolutionary future, as was only to be expected, is that of Peter Drucker. The century's greatest thinker on the age's increasingly dominant social form – management – coined the phrase "knowledge worker" long before others became even remotely aware of the dramatic shift in the nature of work, and the consequences for organisations, as information became the key resource of business and non-profit activities alike.

In his book *The New Realities*, one of his most important contributions to society's awareness of its own development, Drucker forecasts without reservation that "The typical large organisation, such as a large business or a government agency, twenty years hence will have no more than half the levels of management of its counterpart today, and no more than a third the number of managers." Neither the structure nor the problems and concerns, he thinks, will much resemble those of the model, textbook company.

That model was taken from the manufacturing company at the start of the first full post-war decade. That type of business was organised on paramilitary lines: the generals at the top, led by the commander-in-chief, were served by a staff, including specialists in specific areas, who had no direct fighting responsibility; the orders from the top were fed downwards via the staff to the divisional and sub-divisional commanders, each with their own staff functions; these lower ranks in turn instructed the lowest rung of management – the field commanders of the smallest units in which the mass of the paid help congregated.

The term "cannon-fodder" wasn't an unfair description of how the soldiers (for which read workers) were treated. Neither their opinions nor their expertise were consulted: theirs not to reason why, theirs but to do or die. The flow of communication, in military and civilian model alike, was almost exclusively downwards. The upward messages consisted mainly of reports, providing the data which confirmed (or otherwise) that orders had been obeyed, passed on the results, and supplied the information on which the next set of instructions could be based.

To use Drucker's phrase, it was a "command-and-control" model. My own phrase, "order-and-obey", conveys exactly the same reality. In its time, and in its way, the military model worked quite well. But repeated convulsions, both within organisations and in their markets (like, say, those of the Detroit carmakers), showed that the model was getting out of touch with reality and real need long before the information age corroded the principles that held command-and-control and order-and-obey together.

The corrosion stemmed partly from social changes, as individuals began to assert their own rights to participation and equality of voice – not only in business and other organisations, but in the family and society at large. Better education is the prime source of this new assertiveness, reaching its summit in the evolution of new breeds of highly trained specialists – not least in information technology itself – described by Drucker as people "who direct and discipline their own performance through organised feedback from colleagues and customers".

If this resembles anything in the military model, it's the interaction between the staff who served the generals – or the staff who reported directly to the executive directors of the company. The difference is that the new specialists do more than advise: because of the very nature of their specialism, their advice is tantamount to execution. A semi-conductor company's marketing strategy, for example, is inseparable from the ability of its technologists to anticipate and exploit the crucial trends in microelectronics; the management can provide the resources and the knowledge for development and exploitation; it cannot create the opportunity.

The military model early on developed two dominant strains: organisation by function or by product. The former thought of the company as divided into interlocking chunks: one piece consisted of inventing and improving what was to be made; another piece (the largest by far) manufactured the result; and the third distributed the product to the market. Research and development, manufacturing and marketing were alike served and to a great extent controlled by pure head office functions – the administrative departments like personnel and (literally above all) finance.

Functional organisation lost favour for several reasons, springing not from the minds of creative managers, but from the hard realities of commercial life. The heads of the functions were too far away, not just from the customers in the market, but from the managers who were charged with putting policy into practice. Communication between the separate functions was discouraged and slowed down by their very separation. The organogram was orderly, but from the order sprang chaos, in such forms as expensive overlaps, disorganised product ranges, and missed opportunities in markets.

The virtues of the alternative – product-orientation – were rubbed in by the invasion of Japanese companies which, typically enough, had taken the Western model to pieces and reassembled it in more effective form. But the mode has long been familiar: the reduction of central manufacturing and marketing functions to advisory staff only, a divisional structure based on either geography or product group (but often, confusingly, on both), and "strategic business units" (or SBUs) that ostensibly concentrate on a homogenous product line and control all the business functions which are necessary for the success of the line and its commanding SBU.

The problems of separation and communication, though, remained. Functions could still raise barriers between themselves within the units; the latter, moreover, found it even more difficult to talk to each other than had the functional overlords of the past. At a time when many technologies are converging, and at an increasing rate, the difficulties and the dangers are obvious. In the trade-off between discipline and flexibility, the point of balance has been shifting rapidly towards freedom as innovation and creativity have taken precedence over control and regulation.

The answer to a mass of data is not to drown in the sea but to swim by converting the data into keys for action. In any business, the complexity of office work has increased as the power of information, and the need for it, have become more obvious and urgent. Publishing a magazine was once quite simple, for example. The management placed the new product on the market through the usual distribution channels, fixed the price of both magazine and advertising at the going rate, and waited to see if the public would respond. From then on, information processing consisted only of orders and invoices. There was no market analysis, and very little that could have been analysed, in any event.

Today, launches are far too expensive for such simplicity to be afforded. The launch will be preceded by analysis of detailed market information to determine the potential for sales of advertising and copies – if, that is, the magazine isn't being distributed to a "controlled" list, which in its turn demands extremely careful, computerised selection of targeted names. The case for advertising will be backed by further detailed analysis purporting to show the cost-effectiveness of the new medium – and that may need further confirmation by market research after the launch.

The statistical flow, relatively speaking, becomes enormous: management will want and need to know everything from market share and advertisers broken down by type and region to reader response and analysis of editorial costs. Each of these pieces of analysis, moreover, may lead to and influence important management decisions. The company has ceased to be a "thing" business: it has become a "think" business, in which knowledge and decision are twinned.

The move from simplicity to relative complexity has taken place, not only in companies of all shapes and sizes, but within processes. The example which Peter Drucker chooses, investment appraisal, is typical of the whole management process. Drucker has always argued against using a single method of appraisal. But it's no longer enough even to insist on simple payback, the (almost as simple) concept of rate of return and the relatively complex idea of discounted cash flow. As he says, you need those three (but with the present value of all returns discounted through the productive lifetime of the investment), and at least three others.

These are "the risk in not making the investment or deferring it; the cost and risk in case of failure; and finally the opportunity cost – that is, the returns from alternative investments". The importance of the last three has been well known for a long time; mainframes have also been able to work out the complex calculations for many years. But the crucial difference today is that the personal computer, inside an executive workstation or not, can run all the sums at speed, using a proprietary spreadsheet, at that.

The added dimension is that of strategy. Drucker's description – "What was once a budget exercise becomes an analysis of policy" – applies across the board. Management writers have tended to overlook the fundamental importance of the change from historic budgets (comparing latest performance with the same period a year ago) to forecast-based budgets (comparing actuals with forecasts). This converted budgets from an accountant's tool to a management weapon. But the construction and analysis of the forecasts look primitive when set against the permutations and combinations, the testing of assumptions and the analysis of variations, that are now becoming routine.

The shift is one from control to creation. Drucker bases his prediction of massive reductions in the number of "managers" on the disappearance of layers of management. As already noted these tiers exist only as links in the militaristic order-and-obey chain. Continuing with the military theme, one of the prime US defence contractors,

Drucker reports, sought to discover the source, form and flow of the information which its senior corporate and operating managers required for their own functioning.

Possibly six out of fourteen layers were superfluous, it transpired, once the information needs and flows had been co-ordinated. *Prima facie,* if a company has fourteen layers of management, something is grossly amiss; the contrast between General Motors, with its dozen layers, and Toyota, with five, demonstrates that the superfluity is not so much caused by lack of information technology as by poor organisation – for which read basic bad management. The office revolution, though, removes the last shred of excuse for this waste (a waste as much of time as of money).

The revolution makes it possible for complex organisms to imitate simple ones. Paradoxically, the diversified conglomerate, with its many unrelated businesses, is the simple form; the homogenous company (like, say, an oil corporation or an airline) is the complex one. That's because the conglomerate's senior managers take no part whatsoever in operational activity, by inevitable choice. Their only concern is to receive higher and higher profits – whose provision is the concern of the operating managements.

They thus meet Drucker's prescription for the information-based organisation, whose specialists are based in the operations, not at headquarters; which maintain functional staffs in areas like law, public relations, and personnel, but have little or no room for executives who don't execute – "people without operating responsibilities who advise, counsel or co-ordinate". By no coincidence, giant, homogenous oil corporations like Shell were especially prone to breed "co-ordinators": they need do so no longer.

The head office as described above becomes truly the nerve centre of the organisation, the brain which receives all stimuli (data) and actuates all responses. But the senses and powers, the eyes, ears, muscles and the rest of the performing parts, are in the various organs of the body corporate. They are bound together, as are the functions of the human mind and body, by the nervous system – the web of communications. It connects specialists of all kinds with each other, including specialists in "management" – or the art and science of making things happen.

Whether the numbers of these specialists will truly fall is another matter. There could be an analogy with the farm. Look at the numbers employed in what is defined as agriculture: they have fallen astoundingly to only 3% of the US workforce, changing a nation of farmers absolutely into a nation of city-dwellers. Automation, from the combine harvester to the milking machine, has much of the responsibility. But at the apogee of the American farmer, much of the processing of food took place on the farm – and very few people were involved in its marketing.

Today, not only do large numbers labour in all forms of food processing and distribution, but further hordes research into the markets, invent new or allegedly new products, create advertising and promotions. They don't wear overalls, but the output of Madison Avenue copywriters is an extension of the farming industry. By the same token, Drucker's specialists are not "managers". But their work is unquestionably part of what used to be defined as "management". Their needs from the office, however, are different: above all, they do not require its hierarchical functions.

That's because they do not require hierarchy. Hierarchy solves many problems: who gets paid what, who has authority, where the buck stops, and who reports to whom. But as a means of obtaining the best results from people and organisations, it has long been obsolete, and is now positively dangerous, even in the work of non-specialists.

It runs counter to the needs of operating managers charged with running autonomous, discrete units, and to the evolution of outer-directed, faster-moving and flatter organisations, within which specialists can operate in psychological comfort and with practical efficiency. They cannot do so, however, without the office's newly enhanced ability to function as the focus for teamwork and interactive decision-making. And that is the prime reason why the old, familiar office is finally doomed.

Chapter 12

THE MANAGEMENT GAP

The shape and nature of the corporation of the future will determine the physical shape of the office and the nature of the work done by its inhabitants. That is, of course, inevitable. The upwards growth of the "head office", rising like Jack's beanstalk storey by storey, resulted from the pressure of numbers as the specialist departments recruited more and more people. Each group needed a clearly defined floorspace, and the most convenient definition was provided by a single floor.

In that separate domain, if a majority of the workers were clerical or administrative staff, requiring constant supervision as they went about their structured work, large numbers of people could be over-looked from a single vantage point. Office discipline, a *sine qua non* for this kind of output, was greatly facilitated. The separate offices provided for the management, like the special studies reserved for senior boys at a traditional British public school, denoted and reinforced the hierarchy of order-and-obey.

The beanstalk skyscrapers are still rearing up in 1990. But the head office organisations for which they are designed are moving in the opposite direction. Shrinkage is the management order of the day. The trend is nothing new. A building of modest height in Stanhope Gate, headquarters of the General Electric Company, oversees oper-ations many times larger than those for which its three chief constitu-ents, back in the fifties, required all of three much bigger buildings. The current GEC management, moreover, is vastly more effective, too – and it's long been argued (rightly enough) that lean head offices encourage efficiency and fat ones the reverse.

Decimation of head office is the standard technique of corporate raiders, conglomerators and company doctors alike. The pressure for performance and corporate mobility has seen conventional companies slim down several times: the Vickers Tower on London's Millbank still houses the defence and engineering company whose name it bears, and which once occupied all thirty floors: but Vickers today occupies only three. Further up the same thoroughfare, ICI has retained only part of the massive complex which once bore the deadly serious nickname "Millstone House".

In an era of rapidly shifting competition, millstones round the neck will perform their traditional function – they will drown their wearers. Shrinkage in numbers is itself a great leap forward, lowering overheads, shortening lines of communication and forcing work back to where it belongs – in the operating arms of the business. But offices exist on the periphery as well as in the centre. Keeping the number of office workers down is the precondition of the office revolution, and one of its main products: but the revolution itself will require radical reforms.

In *The New Realities*, Peter Drucker has painted a clear vision of the radical company. His head office will contain only the back-up services which the top management requires – legal, public relations, human resources, labour relations and so on. All other specialisms will be located entirely or partially at the operational end of much flatter structures, which means that "the large information-based organisation will more closely resemble the organisation of 150 years ago than today's big companies or big government agencies."

But the Victorian department of state, topped by just two people, the minister and his secretary, with very few chiefs and an army of Indians, gives an upside-down picture of the new organisation. Those few chiefs monopolised knowledge. In Drucker's new company, "knowledge will lie primarily at the bottom", among the Indians, "in the minds of specialists who do different work and direct themselves". Specialists may well cease to be the filling in the sandwich, lying "between top management and the operating people": instead of attempting "to infuse knowledge from the top", managements will have to obtain it from below.

There are plenty of signs that Drucker's vision is already becoming reality. One is the rise of the *ad hoc* group, bringing together people from different disciplines to tackle specific tasks. The task force is a familiar idea from the military model, of course. The difference is the change from emergency use (for example, when a crash programme has to be initiated and executed) to regular employment as a continuous management tool. That becomes inevitable when the full implications of Japanese methodology sink in.

A good Japanese management insists (and has done so for a long time) that all interested parties and disciplines be involved at all times in the creation of new products and plans. The idea of marketing, finance and production acting in isolation is as foreign to this concept as it should always have been in the West. Today, maintaining Western separatism is liable to prove fatal in the marketplace. But if people are constantly working with different associates from different "departments", what significance do the latter have?

Drucker uses the example of research to illustrate the profound influence of what he calls "synchrony", which is replacing "the traditional *sequence* of research, development, manufacturing, and marketing". The very beginning of the project brings together specialists from each part of the former sequence, and the multi-disciplinary approach stays in command the whole way through to completion – and beyond. The advantages are quantitative as well as qualitative: synchrony is one key to reducing the time taken in developing new cars from the old, absurd industry norm of four years.

Apart from their sequential nature, these overlong car programmes conformed to many of the precepts of the new management. Ideally, the project had a clear leader, a product champion who could draw on all necessary resources to bring out the new model on time, on cost and to specification. But the order-and-obey managers at head office maintained close control over programmes vital to a car company's future, and would often override the project team – as when Henry Ford II, according to Lee Iacocca, insisted on a last-minute lengthening of the latter's beloved Mustang.

Is there any intrinsic reason why top managements will accept a true diminution of their powers by total task delegation to teams of specialists – permanent or *ad hoc*? There are plenty of precedents: the treasury specialists, for instance, make vital contributions to profits by their activities in the credit and foreign exchange markets, but very few chief executives seek to exercise any control over their treasurers – or even to understand more than the basics of their work.

Drucker has a dual metaphor for the new role of the chief executive: the head of a hospital, or the conductor of a symphony orchestra. As he notes, hospitals are traditionally divided between specialisms (actually called "firms" in British teaching hospitals) whose leaders are themselves senior specialists. *Ad hoc* teams are quite common – indeed, complex operations like heart transplants are inconceivable without the interaction of several specialisms. However, it can't be said that the hospital chief directs "strategy" – the choice between options, the essence of management elsewhere, may be the essence of patient care, but it doesn't animate hospital management anywhere in the world.

Hospital offices are heavily administrative, and will thus benefit enormously from automation: so will the patients, when (for example) the successes and failures of alternative courses of treatment of all hospitals, across nations and even the world, can be collated and compared at speed. This is a perfect example of how information which at present exists, but cannot be assembled, and cannot therefore be used, will profoundly affect how organisations go about their business. Information technology will also lift much of the administrative load (the "paperwork") which doctors, like policemen, have presently to carry – but for which they are patently unsuited and for which they are not truly being paid.

The hospital analogy, as Drucker himself writes, is less satisfactory than that of the symphony orchestra. There is one conductor, not supported by any subsidiary management, who controls what may be large numbers of individual specialists. The metaphor is brilliant, but stops short of the complex necessities of organisations whose output (unlike that of an orchestra) is not prescribed in advance. The traditional orchestra's work is highly structured: every copy of the score is identical, and every first violin plays the same notes (in theory) as every other first violin.

The scope for variation in interpretation, intonation, tempo, technical skill and so on is large, and that is where the conductor exercises his "executive" powers. He may also (but not necessarily) have heavily influenced the selection of personnel and their collective training. But the chief executive of most organisations is like a conductor who must improvise the symphony as he conducts, leading players who themselves are making up their instrumental parts as they go along. There is some modern concert music of precisely this nature. But the most obvious precedent is jazz, where all is improvisation around a given theme, and where there is no "conductor" – only, at most, a *primus inter pares.*

Firsts among equals were not found in the organisations which Drucker cites as models – like the totally flat structure of the Indian civil service, which ran "the vast and densely populated sub-continent" with no more than a thousand people. Nine provinces were managed by nine political secretaries, each directly commanding district heads whose numbers greatly exceeded modern ideas of "span of control". This only worked because the district officer was confined to four key tasks and reported on a very simple basis.

Each reported every month in writing and "in detail what he had *expected* would happen with respect to each of the tasks, what actually *did* happen, and why the two *differed* if there was a discrepancy". Then he continued the cycle by writing what he expected to happen in the next month and how he would act in consequence, "asked questions about policy, and commented on long-term opportunities, threats and needs". His boss then wrote back full comments on every point.

From these examples, Drucker draws three conclusions about the future, information-based organisation. Its top management must:

1. Set clear objectives for the whole organisation and all its component parts and people.
2. Set up organised feedback that "compares results and expectations so that every member can exercise self-control".
3. Insist that everybody takes "responsibility" for information, answering the two key questions: "Who in this organisation depends on me for what information?", and "on whom, in turn, do I depend?"

The last of the three points restates very emphatically what is thoroughly established as the only sensible or truly effective means of obtaining the best from management information systems, or MIS. The executives responsible for these services have risen quite far up the hierarchy of large companies. But they and their departments cannot predetermine what managers require for the proper execution of their jobs. Drucker rightly castigates them for being "cost centres" rather than "result centres" – for the unifying force behind the companies that will succeed tomorrow is the driving orientation towards results.

The offices of tomorrow, from headquarters downwards, thus become engines for facilitating results, and the head office team itself becomes the chief facilitator. But if you remove the second-guessing and eliminate direct supervision of large management support staffs (which will diminish along with the second guessing), top management numbers themselves must fall. It's conceivable that a large organisation could be headed by the combination of two managing partners and a chief administrator (in the augmented finance director function), with a collection of subsidiary troikas beneath them.

Shortage of top management opportunities is one of the problems that Drucker identifies as the information-based organisation takes over. The difficulty has long been familiar in journalism, where successful troikas of editor, managing director and advertising director left no peaks for the young and ambitious to scale. They necessarily took the door marked exit. The levelling down of hierarchies, however, is to an extent its own cure, since it allows personal distinction (as in medicine) to become what it should always have been, the only true mark of success.

But as the nature and shape of management changes in these ways, what will happen to the nature and shape of the office block? Years ago, a highly imaginative American adman named Marion J. Harper, who was ahead of his time in many respects, set up an advertising company called Jack Tinker Associates, not in an office, but in a Manhattan apartment. It was an attempt to emulate the concept of the "think-tank", which is nothing but an organisation of task forces, and may well be a model for the management of the future.

A think-tank exists, not to gather information, but to assimilate, absorb, conclude and communicate. So does a management as it sets about the task of closing the true management gap – that between the ideal, the standard of high effectiveness, and the real, the sub-performance currently obtained. That's where the information-based company will win; not because information technology will run the company, but because it will provide the tools with which to perform better the vital tasks, ranging from competing to innovation (which is a form of competition).

The offices of small top executive teams, working in groups, using data to define and achieve their objectives, and to analyse and portray reality, are likely to become more and more like think-tanks them-selves; more like apartments; and much less like the skyscraper anthills of the asphalt jungle. As so often happens in human history, that culture may be erecting its largest monuments at precisely the moment when their day is done.

Chapter 13

THE BINDING OF THE BUSINESS

The office revolution, as noted in Chapter 11, carries a threat to one endangered species, threatened with extinction for at least the last half-century, for which no Greenpeace or Worldwide Fund for Nature has taken up the cudgels. That is the middle manager. One problem (as with some other endangered animals) is to find the species in the first place. Presumably, everybody between the shopfloor supervisor and top management is in the middle – but that must mean the great majority of those with any personal responsibility in the organisation.

How can they be threatened without the whole outfit being put at risk? What is this strange plague, anyway? And can it really doom a whole social class to disappearance? The impact of executive information systems on people whose main function is to process information is only one aspect of the deadly murrain in question: the electronic revolution described in these pages. The powers of the computer and its associated hardware and software are now so enormous (and waxing so fast) that, say the prophets of middle management doom, all the routine tasks currently executed by the middlemen will become redundant.

That being so, you can remove the tasks and execute the executants without any effect on the organisation – except, of course, the saving of a whole heap of costs. To take one example, you no longer need a manager standing by to investigate the cause of some plant disorder and rectify it before output shudders to a halt. The chief executive will know about the problem as soon as anybody – the computer will tell him, and will also diagnose the fault and institute the correction before you can say Ned Ludd.

The latter is supposed to have laid into stocking-frames, bequeathing his name to a later generation of Northern rebel workers who in the early nineteenth century set about the machinery that seemingly threatened their jobs. Now, if you believe an account in *The New York*

Times, white-collar Luddites are intent on sabotaging the advance of the new technology for much the same reason.

Thus, Procter & Gamble managers at one ultra-modern plant are said to have ensured that electronic monitoring equipment of the type just described was never linked to head office – and that was five years ago. In the intervening period, however, there's been very little evidence that the new Luddites are on any kind of general rampage, or that deep-laid resistance to computer systems linking the office to the factory will be replicated within the office itself.

Maybe that's because the majority of the majority, so to speak, are not aware that they are living in the Temple of Doom. Or could it be that they have heard, or heard of, this particular cry of "Wolf!" before? At the start of the computer age, the same fears were rampant. Giant computers would create the "total management information systems", mentioned earlier, that would sweep away middle managers like so many cobwebs.

This initial threat foundered on two realities: the giant systems didn't materialise, and the mid-century's many-splendoured expansion and diversification kept on creating work for supposedly idle hands to do. Hundreds of thousands of middle managers did indeed lose their jobs in ensuing years: but not at the hands of the demon information technology. The villain has been good or bad old bureaucracy, aided and abetted by recession and mismanagement.

If a relatively well-managed business like IBM needs to shed 16,000 employees (in the first of a series of such retrenchments), many of them middle managers tempted by early retirement offers which they could hardly refuse, the volume of human silt in other organisations must be enormous. It only takes another crisis (like the squeeze of IBM's profits from the minis and the PC clones) to stimulate a clear-out. After which, of course, the silting up begins all over again. C. Northcote Parkinson long ago charted the process by which administrative empires grow even as their workloads diminish.

The issue is whether information technology's latest leaps forward will bring Parkinson's disease to an end. Certainly IT means that you won't need people whose "main, if not their only function", in the words of Peter Drucker, "is to serve as 'relays' – human boosters for the faint, unfocused signals that pass for communication in the traditional pre-information organisation". It's too fanciful, however, to suggest that awareness of this impending redundancy explains the obstructive attitude of many managers towards the computer in its latest, personal variety.

This has brought the reality of the office revolution on to their own desks, with unquestionable benefit to their ability to perform their

present tasks. Many managers, though, shy away from the things –
and the shyest of all are at the top. The power and beauty of the
executive information system will change this situation. But for a long
time yet the revolution will be obstructed by resistant senior managers
who are less worried about losing their jobs (they are hardly going to
fire themselves) than by the fear that the old dog won't be able to
learn new tricks.

Anyway, he finds the trick somewhat demeaning: keyboards and
screens (even mouse-driven ones), after all, are the tools of typists,
not tycoons. But this is unquestionably a passing phase. A new generation is rising whose keyboards fit their hands like gloves. And many
of their elders are finding (as did Sir John Harvey-Jones and his
fellow directors at ICI in an experience recounted in Chapter 18)
that computerised information systems greatly enhance the directorial
ability to direct. That does have implications for their underlings – it
increases the visibility of their management and its results.

If this in turn robs them of some autonomy, it will fly in the face of
the clear trend (shown at ICI as much as anywhere else) towards
breaking big companies down into smaller, manageable businesses
with a single boss in charge (and in the firing line, so to speak). While
kings in their own kingdoms, these people are obviously part of the
filling in the corporate sandwich. Their jobs would only disappear if
the computerised company found itself able to reverse engines and
centralise.

That was the misplaced dream of twenty-five years ago, however; it's
more likely that the 21st century corporation will use the housekeeping
powers of the computer to free human managers to exercise their
creative, entrepreneurial abilities – but to do so with vastly superior
information and under much more intelligent control. This certainly
implies a reduction in levels of hierarchy, which inevitably means a
cut in the number of hierarchs.

The article cited in *The New York Times*, under the heading "Why
Managers Resist Machines", links this levelling down to the information revolution. It quotes a study of sixty companies which showed
the top performers spending twice as much on information as the
worst: the top dogs, with only four layers of management, had halved
the number needed (or not needed) by the lesser brethren. The *Times*
also quotes a British business – the home electronics division of Thorn
EMI. Here, too, management levels are down to a mere four, which
will certainly be to the taste of those best-selling rebels with a cause,
Robert Townsend and Tom Peters.

But *Up the Organisation*, in which Townsend launched his attack
on the big corporate bureaucracies, antedates the IT era by many

years; in the new Peters work, *Thriving on Chaos*, he abandons his old love of big companies (where *Excellence* is apparently no longer to be found), and sings hosannas to flat hierarchies with few levels. These are not encumbered by what Peters's old firm, McKinsey & Co, detected in a study of advanced manufacturing: "middle managers and support-service layers that clog the wheels of change", and therefore need "clearing out".

The clearing out would be necessary, and the layers superfluous, in any conditions. The information revolution may have made it easier to bypass middle management and achieve results like that at Nucor (greatly admired by both Townsend and Peters), which sells annually more than $750 million of steel with the aid of only seventeen head office employees. But how does this differ from what Sir Owen Green did long ago at the British conglomerate BTR, where a head office of 300 was decimated?

It's been par for the course, ever since Lord Weinstock's magic was applied to the heavily larded General Electric Company, to start turnarounds and takeovers by removing surplus middlemen. (One axeman is supposed to have done the job, brusquely enough, by firing everybody on the left-hand side of the corridor.) The object of such exercises isn't only to save costs – though those of a fully staffed London head office can run into terrifying rows of noughts. When at Rank Xerox in Britain, Paul Allaire, the future instigator of the company's executive support system in the US, reduced the head-quarters division by 40% for a saving of some £150 million.

But the great practitioners of holding company management want more than economy. They want the minimum distance between themselves and the operating executives so that the centre can exert more direct control over the businesses; and so that the business bosses, subject to that control, can get on with the real jobs of management. These maestros hate job titles like "co-ordinator" and organisation charts with the dotted lines that indicate unclear channels of command – in fact, they hate organisation charts. Not so the bureaucrats: Boeing once found "maybe ten people who spent full days working" on the things. The great planemaker faced a very real threat of bankruptcy at the time. Yet "every time someone was promoted, a new chart would be worked up. We decided to do without the charts for a while" – and without the ten chartists, presumably.

That was in 1969, which again makes it clear that overmanning in the middle, just like the accumulation of fat round the managerial midriff, has a cycle independent of information technology. The fat builds up until the victim can't fasten his trousers, financially speaking; a crash diet makes him lean and hungry; and then he starts to eat and fatten up again – unless somebody stops him. And that somebody won't be an information technologist: it will be a determined top manager who sternly resists the build-up of functional fat (including that in IT departments, which can themselves be enormous).

It's not just that excessive functional support services waste money and get in the way. The managerial value of IT lies in generating information which all executives can share as they adopt the collegiate style that ignores layers and produces the free-wheeling, independent-minded collective of the Townsend–Peters ideal. If a company is planning a new model of a product, for example, everybody gets into the act; they can all see the financial implications, the market data, the production consequences, the personnel needs; they can all vary the mix and see what the effect is on the bottom line.

The chief executive can more rapidly approve the final decision, knowing that his managers – even those with major specialist responsibilities – have worked and agreed on the project together, and not in separate compartments. But those managers will still be men and women, not machines; and they will still be somewhere in that elusive middle. Those who best survive a period which will certainly see continued pressure and restraint on middle management numbers will be "holographic" managers, to borrow a powerful metaphor from a Thorn EMI man quoted by *The New York Times*.

By that, he meant generalists operating with "shared information making each person, each part contain the whole". But the driving force that makes the flatter, fast-flowing organisation work will be the bosses at the top. The fact that they will use IT much more vigorously than the also-rans will be a consequence, rather than a cause of their excellence – although IT will in turn contribute powerfully to the latter.

The excellence of those left managing lower down, however, will also hinge on the possession and effective use of information in best Japanese style. Every management technique and method used in Japan can be found in the West – somewhere. But it is not applied consistently or comprehensively enough. You cannot compete with the top of the world class unless marketing, manufacture, finance, R & D, personnel and innovation are all bound together: and what binds them is the information which the office revolution is now making far more effective.

Using this coherent, connected information, middle managers will still play a crucial role in the services which account for the bulk of the modern economy – and for a constantly growing proportion of employment in so-called manufacturing concerns. The immense investment of the banks in automation has been accompanied by a demand for more counter clerks to handle the proliferation of IT-driven "products": the analogy is obvious. But there's an even more fundamental point. Where will top management itself come from? Where will its members gain the necessary experience of managing people, plants, markets, finances and, for that matter, information technology?

They will have to rise to the apex of the pyramid up its slopes; there can't just be an electronic void between the boardroom powerhouse, the plant (even though that will, of course, itself be manned increasingly by robotic machines) and the markets (even though they will, of course, themselves be monitored by electronic supervisors). The endangered species can therefore relax somewhat, partly because no middle would eventually mean no top, either, and, as noted earlier, the last thing top managers are prone to is extinguishing themselves. But there is a more important factor. The main cause of middle management redundancy has been the wasteful cycle of creation, destruction and re-creation of unwanted middle management jobs – and that is a disease which the office revolution is able and going to cure.

Chapter 14

THE NATURE OF BUSINESS

The nature of business management and the development of management technology (for which read "the office") are very closely linked. In the much more stable business environment of the 1950s, corporations achieved success predominantly through their ability to organise and control structured activities. Decisions could be made with what seemed like perfect safety (but was even then illusory in the long term) on the basis of industry experience and individual instinct, or "gut feel". No longer.

The environment for the 1990s, as companies struggle to stay competitive, is both dynamic and unstable. When the nature of business and of competition is changing so rapidly, information systems must keep step. Indeed, it's become a question of which is moving faster – for information technology itself is becoming a competitive weapon of great power. Already, as the unstructured workload has magnified, in both man-hours and importance, the numbers of people required to handle the information in the system have swollen, and so has the pressure to bring the whole process of informing and handling information under full and effective management control.

All this sounds light years away from that calm, deliberate world of the 1950s. Yet in 1958 Harold J. Leavitt and Thomas L. Whisler took a long look forward to 1988. They forecast:

1. A marked change in the role and scope of middle managers as some of 1958's roles became more structured and lost status and reward: while some in-the-middle positions would become more technical and specialised, overall numbers of middle managers would fall as organisation structures flattened out.
2. Top management would assume more responsibility for innovation, planning and creation as the rate of obsolescence and change accelerated: long-term vision would become vital.
3. Recentralisation would become the order of the day as large

organisations took advantage of new information technologies: these would not only improve top management's information, but would tighten its control over decisions made lower down.

When writing, Leavitt and Whisler can't have had much idea of the direction in which information technology was moving – the IT industry itself, after all, was hopelessly wrong in its own horoscope readings much later than 1958. However, the authors rightly saw that the cost of information was tumbling as its provision became more abundant. They thought that decentralisation, the vogue for most of the post-war period, was a response to a size and complexity beyond the grasp of current management armed with current technology. As the latter improved, it was only reasonable to assume that top management would seek to recapture what it had surrendered.

These arguments were recapitulated by three authors – Lynda M. Applegate, James I. Cash, Jnr, and D. Quinn Mills – in a much later article in the *Harvard Business Review* (Nov – Dec 1988). As they say, the Leavitt-Whisler analysis, in many of its elements, now looks very robust. A million managers and staff professionals may have disappeared from corporate America since 1979, thanks (or no thanks) to actions like those of one oil company president: he cut back management numbers by 40% and *afterwards* replaced "the work of scores of analysts and mid-level managers" by a "sophisticated on-line executive information system" (to which he added electronic mail).

Then there's the case of a manufacturer which, in the process of speeding up new product launches, reduced its middle manager ranks by 30%. It used layoffs, divestments and early retirement as it linked its multi-national operations, via "a sophisticated telecommunications network", to "a centralised computer database, which integrated all aspects of the highly decentralised business". Without question, these are only a couple among hundreds of examples where computer systems have "assumed many of the communication, co-ordination and control functions that middle managers previously performed".

Note, however, that the manufacturing company just mentioned was a "highly decentralised" business. There's no hint that electronic restructuring and recentralisation are one and the same thing. Far from it. As the authors point out, Leavitt and Whisler in forecasting tighter top management control "did not anticipate ... that microcomputers would enable simultaneous improvement in decentralised decision-making". The 1988 article believed that the old choice between centralise and decentralise has become obsolete. "Today there is a third option: technology-driven control systems that support the flexibility and responsiveness of a decentralised organisation as well as the integration and control of a centralised organisation."

Can you really have your management cake and eat it? Can you do as well as Leavitt and Whisler at predicting the evolution of management in response to technology – in times of much more rapid change? When IT development times have more than halved in thirty years and are still reducing, the game of telling the future is far more hazardous. The hazards are fewer, however, if the future has already happened. And in the ebb and flow of corporate life in the late 1980s, developing rapidly into the 1990s, the shape of things to come was the shape of things that had already happened.

What does already exist that will be commonplace in 2018 – sixty years on from Leavitt and Whisler? The list includes:

1. Expert systems which substitute for human intelligence in analysing situations and preparing the appropriate response.
2. Very small computers with very great power that can process all the information any manager is ever likely to require at very great speed.
3. Computerised communications networks that can handle computer output, text, images and speech over any number of channels and outlets.
4. To all practical intents and purposes, infinite storage capacity.

The consequences for management and the office of these four knowns, together with the magnification of their contribution by being united in networks, are in themselves profound. To these must be added what can now be assumed (such as the advent of computers that will select from their vast stores of information by association; and that will also question and learn). Such advances will surpass today's relatively primitive expert systems to convert the computer into an extension, not just of man's memory and powers of simple logic, but of human reasoning and intuition.

Applegate, Cash and Mills speculate interestingly about current research into "electronic brainstorming, group consensus and negotiation software, and general meeting support systems". They also mention "electronic communication software and applications that make communication and the exchange of documents faster and easier". Such aids to group working – which these authors see as the dominant trend of the future – will speed up and facilitate what already exists. But what has not been envisaged by today's forecasters? What is the equivalent of the microcomputer, unsuspected by Leavitt and Whisler in 1958?   The question is intimidating to anybody attempting to assess how management will respond. The result could be very similar to the process that has affected virtually all markets: fragmentation. Just as markets have split into segments, so management could become much more diverse, much more varied in form, much less susceptible to generalisation. This "anything goes" conclusion certainly fits with the Applegate group's forecasts on organisational structure. They believe that:

1. Companies will have the benefits of small scale and large scale simultaneously.
2. Even large organisations will be able to adopt more flexible and dynamic structures.
3. The distinctions between centralised and decentralised control will blur.
4. The focus will be on projects and process rather than on tasks and standard procedures.

If this sounds like the best of all possible worlds, the authors won't argue with the interpretation. They see the technology as the answer to "the challenge to make large companies, with their economies of scale and other size advantages, as responsive as small ones". Technology will, in this vision, remove the barriers to innovation: the layers of management, the long lines of communication, the compartmentalisation of expertise, and the inertia bred by all three. Hierarchy and the matrix organisation will go out of the window as the "adhocracy", the "network organisation", or the "cluster" take over.

The last term is favoured by the authors: all three, however, are different ways of looking at organisations which are "fluid and flexible", in which people come together for specific purposes, and part when these are fulfilled, to join other groupings – all within a framework that holds these separate efforts together and drives them towards a common end. There can't be much argument that here, as usual, the technology is appearing just when it is most needed. For example, the number-crunching computer appeared just when the progress of large organisations and major projects would have been impossible without it.

The technology of dispersed management control and group working has developed at exactly the moment when marketing and human forces are causing companies to implode. The trend towards the use of task forces parallels the break-up of companies into discrete units under separate and truly responsible management – and also parallels the break-up of corporations into genuinely separate companies at the bidding of corporate raiders and buy-out leaders.

The central management of very large companies has been having a hard time proving that it genuinely "adds value". Instead, the assumption is that almost any degree of centralisation *subtracts* value – that the independent parts are worth more than the stock market value of the whole because, as independent units, their value (and not just in stock market terms) actually *is* greater. By encouraging discrete local managements, the corpocrats have only made their own impotence more obvious. Will this condition now be much improved by the corpocrats' escape from their own "insulation from operations"?

More and more of the information "they need to monitor, co-ordinate and control their businesses" will be at their fingertips. They won't have to wait "for the analysts and middle managers to prepare reports at the end of a prolonged reporting period". On the contrary, with immediate feedback, "managers will be able to adjust the strategy and tactics as circumstances evolve rather than at fixed time intervals. And if a change ... is warranted, advanced communications technology will send the message to employees promptly." To put it gently, that doesn't sound like decentralisation: more like the recentralisation foreseen by Leavitt and Whisler.

The more sophisticated the office technology becomes at presenting information in assimilable form, the greater the temptation for higher levels of management to justify their own roles by intervening – or interfering – not just in decisions, but in their execution. Power in organisations tends to rise to the top, not fall to the bottom. Information is power, true, and the more that it accumulates in the hands of sub-managers and professionals, working in groups, the stronger their ability to make creative decisions. But where does decisive power rest? Applegate, Cash and Mills believe, and rightly so, that the quality of decision-making will be improved greatly by deeper understanding of its nature as "sophisticated expert systems and knowledge bases" help to capture "decision-making processes". But will everything actually become so much easier in the way they foresee? They note, again rightly, that "sophisticated business analysis and simultaneous models will help ... analyse business situations and recognise the consequences, thereby decreasing and managing risk."

It's hard not to feel, though, that these authors, themselves loving the concepts of group working and of freeing managers for creativity, have modelled their view of the future as much on their hopes as their analysis. The advances they enumerate are required because business is becoming more difficult, not easier: the number of variables is increasing all the time (for instance, as markets fragment), and competitive advantages can be eroded as fast as they are created. All the new technology can promise (more than promise, for it also delivers) is to turn the office, and the management processes inside the office, from data-processing facilities to engines of applied information.

Instead of the office controlling its inhabitants, they will have the power to control the office. But the technological advance is setting the scene for a new battle for power of a different sort – between the higher directorate of organisations and the "fluid and flexible" elements that, in the last analysis, those above set in place and provide with resources. The old decisive (and divisive) issues of who gets what money, and who doesn't, won't be removed by expert systems and artificial intelligence. Nor will either the people in the marketplace, or in the organisation itself, be wholly amenable to reason.

The hope must be, however, that greater transparency and sounder decision-support systems will greatly encourage the outburst of delegated creativity that the Applegate group expects. But major corporations will not exploit these new strengths without upheaval. After all, the first thirty years of the IT revolution saw a waning of the relative powers of the large Western corporations, though not of the abilities of individual managers within them. The process of erosion was based on socio-economic and technological developments, and on that basis erosion is likely to continue; for the new technology, unless used with exceptional creativity, further reduces the advantages of economies of scale.

In the large factory, flexible manufacturing, allowing short runs at economic cost, is the answer to fragmenting and more complex demand – but in many industries the small manufacturer can also use advanced technology to meet or beat the large firm on costs. In the office, information technology, allowing much more effective, dispersed use of the large corporation's huge resources of information, is an answer to dispersal in the more complex marketplace. But the same office revolution means that the small competitor can now nearly match the giant in the strength of its decision support and communications systems.

In short, the challenge to management in large organisations isn't to make them behave more like entrepreneurial small companies, but to make them truer to their own true strengths – to make them look *outwards* to the markets where they have immensely strong positions in terms of size and customer franchise, and *inwards* to the ranks of talented people that they have always been able to recruit. The office revolution does indeed give management the opportunity to reverse bureaucratisation: it doesn't follow that the opportunity will be seized without effort.

Chapter 15

THE DEVELOPMENT OF THE DESKTOP

The workstation offers the beginning of hope for white-collar productivity. Cynics about the productive potential of office automation
must have received reinforcement from the disappointment recorded
between 1978 and 1985, when output per white-collar worker appears
to have fallen slightly. Improved organisation of work alone should
have generated gains. On the face of it, therefore, the technology of the
period in which personal computers invaded desks in their hundreds of
thousands was counter-productive.

The excuse for this poor performance is a good one. The first PCs
were not only used for limited purposes – apart from word processing,
only two or three other programs were generally even purchased – but
stood alone. The repository of corporate data remained the
mainframe. Even if its custodians had been willing to share its secrets
with the desktops, they lacked the technical means. Local area networks (LANs) and essential hardware and software were the missing
links. They are no longer missing.

Since the mid-eighties, networking the desktops has been a matter
of will, not means. Yet the research group IDC could report that in
1988 Britain's offices housed 2.4 million business computers which
still stood alone, unconnected to any network. John Kavanagh, writing
in *Finance* magazine, noted that this represented an investment of
around £6 billion: by definition, most of that vast sum must have
been spectacularly underused. The year before, according to another
researcher, Intelligent Electronics, only 8% of all the PCs in the world
were networked.

Nor will the gap between actual and potential be closed at any early
moment. The same researcher predicts that less than a quarter of PCs
will be connected by 1991. True, that's a trebling in four years,
which represents tremendous growth – the Logica systems group sees
European expansion of LANs running at 36% per annum compound
between 1988 and 1994, when over half a million networks will be

operating. But the growth is misleading, for many of these computer weddings will only be marriages of convenience – arranged to share printers and high-capacity data storage discs rather than to revolutionise the office.

That revolution demands successful communication of office output by electronic distribution throughout a planned network. The demands on the network are clear. It must handle all the characteristics of the compound document without degradation. In addition, network-wide quality printing devices must allow choice of output devices and speeds as well as the capability to view all information via the workstation. The latter must be fully integrated with the system to allow easy access and a working view on an "electronic desktop" designed to give very easy interchange of information.

The electronic display now plainly winning the market battle takes the form of "what you see is what you get", which ensures consistency of illustration both electronically and when printed, to facilitate the understanding of the information illustrated. In other words, the network consists of integrated intelligence. Integrated and integral are the key words. Kavanagh quotes a British manager at Digital Equipment, who says rightly that "Personal computers must be treated as *integral* components [my italics] of a company's overall information technology strategy."

He goes on to point out that "Huge investments in self-contained personal computers are simply not economically viable." Suiting the action to its words, Digital in 1989 was running a $14 billion business with 130,000 users tied together by work stations, minicomputers and superminis – with not a mainframe on the hundreds of office premises. Since the company is the largest manufacturer of minis, its aversion to mainframes is understandable. But there's no doubt that the role of the central computer is changing rapidly – and, indeed, is moving rapidly downwards in status.

As Kavanagh wrote, "There is growing support for the view that the big central mainframe is now only one component in a corporate network, perhaps used simply for managing the central company database, rather than being the main processing machine for all departmental and subsidiary systems." Far beyond the sharing of printers lies the total corporate information strategy – a grand phrase. But what are the practical stages of its implementation, and what are the costs?

Peat Marwick McLintock did a study for a large retailer, Computerland, that isolated four distinct stages in the evolution of information strategy:

The Development of the Desktop

1. The data processing era.
2. The task automation stage.
3. The process transformation stage.
4. Business transformation.

In the first of these stages, the company gets interested in the new technology, generally because a few staff are taken with its attributes, and the cost is usually low: so, of course, are the payoffs. But the company has embarked on a process in which, say the consultants, costs increase "dramatically", while at the same time business benefits rise "at an exponential rate".

The first demonstration of this truth is provided by the second stage: the point beyond which, as this book is written, only a minority of organisations have progressed. "Task automation" involves using PCs to raise productivity in repetitive work previously done manually. According to one of the Computerland report's authors, "Most organisations have reached a plateau at the top of phase two. Many now face the migration to the next phase – which involves a number of fundamental changes in spending, in benefits potential, and in management."

This process transformation phase is governed by the realisation that, since individuals seldom work in isolation, neither should their office equipment. In any office, individual tasks contribute to a larger whole, and the total effort is directed towards some corporate aim. To quote a Peats man, Geoff Jarvis, "Information technology is increasingly seen as providing the opportunity for organisations to change the way processes are carried out and to improve the linkages between the individual tasks which make up the process."

As this book emphasises, desktop computing can't unleash personal creativity in this way without changing the organisation structure and the working life of the management and the office. Peats has identified significant hidden expense in changes to working practices and organisation structure that take the costs far beyond those involved in the equipment and programs which create a networked system. The countervailing argument, in Jarvis's words, is that the "benefits are likely to be in orders of magnitude because of the changes they make possible in the economics of the business".

That leaves the vital question of the likeliness of that "likely". The cost-benefit sums are tough enough at this third stage; but the complexity increases with the fourth, "business transformation" phase. Here, the company radically alters the way in which it goes about its business. This is the stage of strategy where spending on personal computing may well rise with more sophisticated usage; but in which, because of networking, it will be meaningless to separate out elements of an IT bill whose benefits will not be solely financial.

"The strategic use of information technology offers significant business gains, but also involves taking high risks," thinks Jarvis. He lists among strategic and non-financial benefits such highly desirable ends as improving market share or keeping the highest calibre staff, and claims that "the technology can also offer an opportunity to venture into completely new business areas." In this phase, he says, Peats has seen returns that even outstrip those of between 200 and 500% at the process transformation stage.

Managements are bound to be highly sceptical of such high figures based on such generalised arguments. In the past, scepticism has found evidence in the reluctance of those peddling IT dreams to take their own medicine. Now the evidence works in the opposite direction. The suppliers are leading the movement towards computers on every desk, linked with every other computer in the organisation, and used for purposes that leave task automation in its proper place – as a relatively primitive stage in the evolution of the office culture.

It isn't just the hardware suppliers who are changing the way in which they do business. Touche Ross, the accountants and management consultants, started with its national accounting and auditing department, linking computers from four manufacturers over a Torus Systems local area network. The success achieved was high enough to set other Torus projects going, with the initial aim of bringing together word processing, spreadsheet modelling, electronic mail, retrieval of technical information and access to the central mainframe.

The reported results are not in the 200 to 500% bracket, but are still impressive. Only a quarter of users failed to improve productivity. Among the great majority whose productivity rose, partners reported 5% gains, managers 10%, secretaries 13% and programmers 25%. Two-thirds of the partners and secretaries thought that their own gains justified the costs; so did 85% of the managers, and all of the programmers.

The costs, however, were substantial. Excluding the PCs themselves, the organisation spent £1,500 a head: meaning that, for an office staff of 1,000, the impressive sum of £1.5 million would be spent over and above the desktop hardware itself. The expenditure does have the immediate benefit, however, of increasing the notoriously low utilisation of the hardware. Kavanagh writes that "partners and managers more than doubled the time spent using IT for productive tasks."

While this still came to only 15% of their working hours, there's little doubt that this proportion rises as habits change. Touche's senior people began to use their PCs to produce finished documents. Once you get used to handling a keyboard for writing and editing, the process becomes more and more automatic. It cuts down the time which the originator need spend on the document, and it saves all the time previously required by secretaries. Touche's found particularly marked gains among novices and relative novices. They had spent a quarter of their time writing memos and reports and giving dictation: that fell dramatically to 7%.

At Peat Marwick McLintock, another physician prepared to heal itself, £2 million and eight man-years were the price for a project linking 250 PCs to a powerful Digital mini across five London sites, each with its own local area network. The scheme, with a target of over 380 computers at eight sites, comprises seventeen standard programs, including individual databases, word processing, office automation and information management via the mini. Like the computers, the software products, bought from different suppliers, all work together as true integration demands.

Even though 90% of Peats' users already had personal computers, stand-alone machines using different packaged programs cannot match the performance of this kind of network. Almost four-fifths of staff thought, some (25%) of them strongly, that the new system had improved their efficiency. Higher job satisfaction was mentioned by 70% of users. Much to the point, nearly half said that they could now spend more time on fee-earning work.

However many pinches of salt are taken, the results of the Touche and Peats cases are consistent with common sense. There are some cautionary notes: in the Touche survey, entitled *Benefits of Technology for Professional Staff*, it was noted that "one or two" people reported "lower initial productivity as they went through the learning curve of mastering the application software. This change is about on a par with other studies conducted by IBM" – and demonstrates the importance that "user-friendly" software is bound to assume in realising the office revolution.

Another relevant point is that people given their own computers benefited more than those compelled to share. The PC, as its name announces, is a personal tool which, paradoxically, produces its greatest benefits by being pooled with others. That principle hasn't yet taken these two firms of accountants and consultants to the final stage of transforming their businesses. But the transition from *"ad hoc* purchasing of self-contained personal computers to a proper strategy of integration" is complete.

Kavanagh goes on to quote the overall moral of these stories from Jarvis of Peats. Pointing out that European spending on desktop computers has more than trebled in six years, Jarvis says that this level of expenditure and growth makes it management's "duty to understand the effect the personal computer's presence has on the organisation and to consider the opportunities it offers for business gain". The white-collar productivity that had responded so sluggishly by 1988 is only the beginning: the end is something far more fundamental to the life and results of the organisation.

BOOK IV
The Progress of the Office

Chapter 16

THE INFORMATION-INTENSIVE COMPANY

The impact of networked office technology on office work itself is only beginning to be felt: but already the results are striking. At Peat Marwick McLintock, the integration, say, of word processing and electronic mail with a database on past experience in the firm and on individuals' expertise may not add up to much on paper (not exactly the *mot juste* since the essence of the exercise is to replace paper by electronics). But in practice integration has had results like those reported to John Kavanagh by Peats' partner Michael Brignall:

"We have a big information flow, a great deal of interaction between consultants who work together yet travel a lot. We waste a lot of time as people move between buildings for meetings or to compare notes on reports or to get proposal reports checked. In some cases people out on client projects were coming to the office just to get reports typed or gather information. Now they can do all this themselves through word processing, electronic mail and central information access."

Precise benefits noted by the beneficiaries include:

1. Taking only two hours to put together a proposal that involved four consultants and secretaries working simultaneously.
2. The ability to complete projects in which a high level of analytical work was carried out by several people working in parallel.
3. When a client arrived at short notice, producing details of similar jobs and consultants with relevant skills in ten minutes.

The results of such sharp changes in basic organisational ability affect all staff, right up to the chief executive – since he can now obtain, sometimes instantly, and very possibly without any intermediary, responses that previously took time: much of which might be spent hunting down the right source. But the most striking cultural change wrought by the revolution surely affects the secretary: in all three examples just mentioned, one result was a major saving in secretarial services.

This doesn't imply the disappearance of the secretary along with the paper to which much secretarial work ministers. This post will remain a pivotal role in the office. But its occupant, almost always female, often highly intelligent and well-educated, has been misused for most of office history, and for most of the available hours, as a mere human extension of the telephone and the keyboard. Very senior secretaries were often, in effect, given secretaries of their own, who could work the keyboard while their senior acted more nearly in a far more valuable role as extension to her boss – personal assistant (PA).

The desktop revolution performs the same function for all secretaries. The human interface is no longer needed between manager and keyboard. The secretary at the keyboard herself uses programs to fulfil tasks which leave the clerical task behind and move towards the executive role – helping the manager to manage more effectively. The consequences must be far-reaching. Secretaries will need a higher level of education and training, and their career paths will more easily lead upwards. The secretary turned top manager, that occasional corporate phenomenon in the past, will be a genuinely and more generally attainable ambition in the future.

The new secretarial role will be partly to facilitate and enhance the process of understanding, which is developed through establishing relationships between available pieces of information; through "browse and discover" searches through files and directories; and through the availability of interchange and exchange of views and opinions. These are actually the functions that the paper-shuffling secretaries of the past performed: arranging a meeting makes possible interchange and exchange of views and opinions, and taking the minutes has been an essential part of the process.

True Office Systems Technology can move the secretary beyond this stage, which will now be handled by the system, to using the latter herself, acting as the eyes and ears of the management position to which the PA is attached. The transformed secretary will inevitably know more about the business, which means that the contribution which can be made must be greater. Numbers, of course, will be fewer: first because so much less clerical work needs to be done, second because there will be fewer executives needing assistance – and the numbers will get fewer still as the potential of networks increases.

On the near horizon looms the full start of the age of expert systems and artificial intelligence. The system will be able to examine relationships and do a logical check for matches and coherence. Arguments to support a point of view can also be built by using logical relationships provided by expert systems whose general availability is only two or three years down the road. Artificial intelligence is the next great step forward in a process of acquiring information which is undergoing truly fundamental and irreversible change.

The mixing of both data and document handling, in both electronic and physical form (which requires scanning, creation, storage and document management), has established a new overall requirement for (1) access to internal and external databases, and a gateway to whatever systems they are on; and (2) gathering information from documents whether or not they have electronic masters. Previous chapters have already discussed the consequences in general terms. Specifically, full office systems are following these patterns:

1. Where information is already held in electronic form, it is accessed through a local area network, with file servers used to browse and gather information; if not, a scanning or imaging device provides the access.
2. In the imminent future, compound documents will include voice as well as graphics, text and data; already the system of today must allow for this development of tomorrow.

What else will the future hold? John Marsh, managing director of CGS (UK), writes that "From the technical standpoint, some broad directions of ... evolution are known today: parallel processing, pattern recognition, knowledge bases, universal networks." He concludes that "expertise is going to be required more than ever before" in installing systems. While advances in software engineering are likely to be startling, Marsh believes that "even a complete elimination of the program coding phase for routine applications will not reduce the need for expertise".

That may be true enough. But paradoxically, as the level of technological wizardry becomes higher and more abstruse, so the ability of the non-technical user to enjoy its fruits is becoming greater – and possibly at a faster rate. That's because it requires intense sophistication of hardware and software to achieve simple use of highly advanced capabilities.

Take the boardroom. As Philip Jordan, managing director of Thorn EMI Computer Software, observed in an article in *Finance* magazine, "Until very recently the use of computers in major corporations stopped well short" of this holy of holies. "Walking through the sales and purchasing divisions or even the distribution departments of large corporations, one would expect to see the customary banks of terminals ... At senior executive level, however, with the exception

119

of the secretarial personal computer for word processing and the odd desktop machine for the rare executive who liked to run his or her own spreadsheet, computers tended to be conspicuous by their absence." The change which Jordan now discerns has given "the boardrooms of a few UK corporations a distinctly high technological feel ... Board meetings ... are illustrated by computer-generated graphics called up by the click of a simple pointer."

Brilliant technological progress was needed to advance beyond the static 35mm slide to these active displays which can be altered at will to incorporate new data and new assumptions. Any information held within the company on its markets and competitors can be called up. "At the press of a button, directors can zoom in on exceptions to the norm and examine the underlying schedules. Trends and patterns in the figures can be seen at a glance from neat, colour-coded graphs."

As Jordan points out, this represents a great shift from the long-established relationship between the computer specialist and the senior executive. No longer is it true that "Other people used the system, the board controlled costs and gave strategic direction." The work of the specialist experts has delivered computing power into the hands of the senior user, who from then on exercises user control: he subsumes some of the expert's previous work, just as, when using the keyboard, he subsumes some of the secretary's.

The result is to strike paper-based reports, and the man-hours used to compile them, from the system. Not only is the time required by paper lengthy, it is often wasted: as Jordan says, "all too frequently the questions the reports were designed to answer have changed in nature, been resolved or given way to others before they arrived." Timeliness is of the essence, as any boardroom habitué knows: business is a state of flux, and issues that seemed urgent at last month's board have receded in importance, to be replaced by others.

The urgency may, in fact, have been real, and the superseded issue may still be eating away, like a canker, at the roots of the business. Inability to obtain information fast enough, however, has shelved the issue before resolution has even begun. The trouble lies partly in the vast and perpetually increasing accretion of data within the organisation and within its markets or areas of operation. Paper is a clumsy means of finding that information, and presenting the data in a structured fashion.

Furthermore, the work of chasing up links and cross-references between what Jordan describes as "multiple sets of paper-based reports" is difficult at best and laborious at all times. Calls for yet another "summary level report" are usually the answer: but these provide no opportunity for executives to dive below the surface, and may, by simplification and omission, stay on the surface – literally superficial.

Recently a survey of executives in the *Fortune* 500 revealed their main complaints about paper-based management reporting systems. The five main, linked complaints, as summarised by Jordan, were:

1. There is simply too much information in the system, so that acquiring relevant information takes too long.
2. Most of the information actually presented to executives is irrelevant.
3. What valuable information executives do receive is in raw form, making it difficult to discern trends, ratios and other important relationships.
4. Data typically arrives without commentary or explanation from those peer executives who are best able to clarify the data.
5. Calling for new or modified reports requires substantial support from information services and takes too much time.

As the account of executive information systems in Chapter 18 emphasises, technology has made all five problems anxieties of the past. The boardroom equipment mentioned above is at the summit of a revolution that extends all the way down the corporation as each executive is freed to tap the same basic resources as the men at the top. Many deeply entrenched habits are attacked on the way – from the use of secretaries as intermediaries to the proprietary attitude towards data which is "owned" by departments or their leaders.

Jordan's recommended way round this obstacle – one as old as corporate time – is to display the name of a "data sponsor" (the board-level director given ultimate responsibility for executive information), together with "flags" indicating "whether or not there are any special textual notes appended to the data". He claims that incorporating traditional patterns in this way "makes a virtue out of what previously might have been an obstacle to the free passage of information".

What's certain is that withholding or manipulating access to information for negative, obstructive or self-serving ends becomes infinitely more difficult: "No one 'owns' the data any more." Jordan uses the word "free" to describe the results. "Open" is perhaps better. What begins as a simple improvement of basic office efficiency by eliminating layers of intervention, automating procedures and facilitating interchange develops into a strategic tool from board level downwards and ends as the means of an open system of management, in which everybody, from secretary upwards, can participate.

Today's necessity is to decentralise success, shifting away from the interior to the exterior, from the centre to the periphery. Genuine success for a genuinely autonomous business with genuine resources at its genuine command relies heavily on excellent information to combine control with freedom. It's impossible to run the flat, fast company without superb information systems. The information intensive philosophy involves defining business objectives and operating to meet them: identifying market opportunities and concentrating efforts to achieve planned business results; having a clear understanding of money and its use as a corporate resource; and having good information systems in support of good decision-making procedures.

Finally, it means organising management to operate as a team – for group or collective working has taken over from lines of command. If that sounds like a Utopian ideal, it is the path which writers like Robert Townsend of *Up the Organisation* and Thomas J. Peters, in the years after *In Search of Excellence*, have been urging. When Townsend wrote, few managements had the will and none had the means. The means of open, interactive management have now been provided by technology. The will has to be provided by management itself.

Chapter 17

THE TOTAL OFFICE PROCESS

Shoshana Zuboff's *In the Age of the Smart Machine* is an important, enlightening and extensive study of the impact of the electronic revolution on people at work, in the office and the plant. The top-down systems she describes, however, are all large-scale endeavours to cut costs by substituting electronic intelligence for human hands and minds. But the true revolution is really being led from below, and in much smaller organisations than those Zuboff studied.

Take Donald F. Tuline, president of Richmond Savings Credit Union in British Columbia. His organisation had only six offices – but networking provided its salvation after a corporate financial crisis, as long ago as 1983. *Business Week* reports that Tuline decided "to attract new business by charging for service according to a sliding scale that gave increasing discounts to his highest volume customers". Because Tuline was in no financial position to pay for a new mini-computer system to do the job, he had his 250 tellers linked up on personal computers. Since start-up in late 1987, service revenues have risen by some $429,000: a very fair return on the $1 million investment.

That in turn was 30% less than the mini-alternative – and the costs keep coming down. *Business Week* quotes the following simple costs for a network of twenty workstations using personal computers, as compared to terminals linked to a mini or mainframe – assuming the same workload on similar jobs and equal training time and productivity gains. The numbers work out at $95,000 for a PC network; $300,000 for the mini-based alternative; and no less than $6 million for the mainframe route.

For flexibility as for cheapness, the PC has the inside track. Tuline's system "writes custom software for itself, helps customers with their tax returns, and does its own direct mail promotions". And, of course, the PCs also carry out the tasks which in 1989, six years after Tuline's inspiration, were still their dominant use in most businesses: office work, above all word processing. Given these advantages, it's surprising that the computer industry's thinkers haven't fully taken on board the huge implications for sales of large computer systems. There are, of course, vested interests at stake – intellectual ones as well as financial. But the writing is on the wall.

Sales growth for mainframes costing more than $1 million, serving over 128 users, was still over 8% in 1988, according to International Data Corporation. The rate is now plummeting, however, and little growth can be anticipated in the early nineties. Minis priced between $100,000 and $1 million, with 17 to 128 users, were expected to peak in 1990 at a 6% growth rate, which already looked optimistic before the year began. At the same time the five million or so PCs attached to installed networks throughout the world in 1989 will be accelerating towards thirty million as the year 1992 comes to an end.

In 1988, Dataquest figures recorded an 85% jump in network hardware and software sales to $4.8 billion. The 15% of America's 40.1 million PCs that were linked in 1989 are only a beginning. By 1992, International Data expects 60.1 million desktop computers to be in operation – and nearly half of then will be networked. Far more important, where today's networks are mostly doing nothing much more than helping users to share an expensive printer, tomorrow's will do everything that Tuline's network does – and more.

The magazine has a five-point account of "the versatility of PC networks" which translates into five questions for top management to answer as it enters the era of office systems technology.

1. Do you want to make it easier for your people to communicate by computer?
2. Do you want to save time (or increase effective employee hours, at no greater employment cost) by reducing the number of meetings and making it possible for several of your staff to work simultaneously on the same problem?
3. Do you want generally to increase the information available inside the organisation, while at the same time making it more digestible – and increasing the company's reaction speed and competitive prowess?
4. Do you want a better return on your IT investment by expanding the combined powers of your computers to grapple with new tasks?
5. Do you want to reduce software costs by stopping people from buying copies of the same programs?

It's very hard to believe that many managers will say no to any of the five questions. Until now, they have had some excuse (though a poor one) in that software and hardware development has lagged behind need, especially for companies already locked into configurations dating back to an earlier age. The industry's giant, IBM, only announced the software packages that make it possible for its PCs, minicomputers and mainframes to "share information easily and work together on computing tasks" as late as May 1989. But that announcement, and the $500 million, two-year development programme that preceded it, are the clearest possible evidence of how sharply the computer age has changed course.

A Motorola vice-president had it exactly right. "We're talking about a world that's totally interconnected," he told *Business Week*. "We will take it for granted – the way we do the phone today." The magazine gives a hard-fact example – a sales manager working on a quarterly budget who can in seconds call up a particular salesperson's results from the previous quarter and insert them into the spreadsheet in exactly the right place, with no need to involve anybody else.

These actually routine transactions will become just that – routine, just as the Motorola man said. Behind the routine, however, lies a brilliant quantity of software, extant and still to come. Like all revolutions, that in the office has burst on to the world before it's complete. There are companies in every country – software and hardware suppliers alike – working away to make networks more effective, to act as "agents" (automatically compiling and distributing up-dates as new data arise), translating a spreadsheet from one supplier into the language of another, making any information available anywhere in the network available everywhere else.

"Groupwire" is an evolution of electronic mail that brings together a group of co-workers via their calendars, scheduling their meetings and tracking their projects. Impacts on the way in which companies are managed are inevitable as electronic memos and position papers flicker back and forth. According to *Business Week*, "Companies say that E-mail eliminates some meetings and makes those that are necessary more productive, since participants can confer electronically beforehand."

The impact has brought more democracy to Mrs Fields, the cookie shop chain, rather than intensifying the isolation which Zuboff's book suggests as a danger. The 650 shops have no paperwork other than government forms and need only 114 staff at HQ, which the chief executive, Randall K. Fields, estimates at a fifth the number of a conventional organisation. "Many companies would not want someone at the first level to be able to send messages to the chairman of the board," says Fields. The electronic suggestion box makes that not only feasible, but normal.

In those organisations where networks have already become a way of business life, developments include:

1. The use of electronic mail to exchange ideas and information on personal and social topics.
2. Evolution of codes to convey nuances like winks and frowns.
3. As at Mrs Fields, encouragement of contributions from workers down the corporate scale.
4. Major savings on costs through streamlining and co-ordinating operations.

On the last point, *Business Week* cites savings of between $1 million and $2 million annually at Coca-Cola Foods, which uses a network database progam "to schedule and monitor production in seven plants across the US". More interesting in terms of the potential of networking is the work done on automating the accounting system. From forty types of spreadsheets, the company has come down to a couple. "We've given 25% of the time back to our financial analysts," says an executive. "How do you put a dollar value on that?"

You probably don't – or rather, can't. Nor can you value the worth of having PCs used instead of idle – for there's no doubt that, as at Coca-Cola Foods, networking greatly encourages the use of the machines. It's like the difference between having a telephone that can only dial one or two numbers and an instrument that can connect to any number you want. Which phone will get more intensively used?

Emerging from the relative shadows of stand-alone hardware into the sunlight of full Office Systems Technology has a very clear objective and pay-off: improving the effectiveness of unstructured work. The technical strength of the development is that it doesn't so much supplant office automation – or applying technology to discrete activities – as build on that earlier stage. Much of the hardware and the infrastructure will already be in place: the idle PCs, the underutilised cabling, the banks of underexploited data. Order entry, inputting data to the computer system, simple text-editing and so on continue: but all these lower-order activities now contribute to the higher-order work that constitutes the overall process of the office and of management.

The company is on the way towards completion of the total office process, which emerges as six interlocking elements: *reprographics* (which covers stand-alone to high volume machines); *word processing* (on a multi-function work station, personal computer or electronic typewriter); *electronic printing* (typically decentralised); *document management* (the ability to file, access and change documents); *electronic publishing* (a very important element, because it allows more effective communication of output); and, finally, *integrated office systems*, including a network architecture that can handle these requirements.

The Total Office Process

Business Week suggests a simple litmus test to find out whether the office is already overripe for the move onward from lower order to this higher realm of integrated systems which can embrace each and all of the six elements. *Do your employees spend more time swapping discs and trying to locate data than working on their spreadsheets?* The advance into new territory begins with buying a local area network, so that the PCs can communicate with each other, and a wide-area network if you want to go off-site. Software costs come down if you buy network versions of the standard programs required – which should include programs for finding lost or damaged files.

The magazine stresses the crucial importance of training for all users, and makes the vital point that bottom-up participation is vital. Thus, a teller at Richmond Savings Credit Union was made the key workgroup figure in establishing part of the system. "Giving an identified process champion time to work with others will improve acceptance of the system and may lead to good ideas on how to use it." The teller customised the software, giving each of 250 work stations immediate access to the financial records of 40,000 customers.

In this flowering new world, thorny problems abound. Many will have to be solved by a network manager who looks after the system and its maintenance day by day, provides back-up and recovery, is in charge of the training and (a highly sensitive issue) controls security. The role of the industrial spy or saboteur is obviously made easier by the very dissemination of information on which Office Systems Technology rests. Unauthorised people can hack into the system; authorised staff can get hold of information you would prefer kept from them; by accident or design files can be altered in ways that weren't intended, by people who weren't supposed to see them.

The bigger the network, says a security expert at Deloitte Haskins & Sell, the bigger the risk. A nice balance has to be struck between providing the freedom of access and exchange without which the network loses its point and ensuring that inadequate security doesn't undermine the company's business. Some safeguards are obvious enough, like restricting night-time access, but far more will be needed – preferably in the interests of genuine security, and not in those of rearguard actions fought by defenders of the informational *status quo*.

The defenders exist at all levels. You would suppose that airline staff, having been used to reservation networks for years, would adapt with particular ease. But according to *Business Week*, at American Airlines "there's fear of resistance as the airline installs a $150 million network that will computerise every job down to the baggage handlers trying to re-unite passengers and their lost luggage." Wayne Pendleton, managing director of American's Sabre Computer Services division, told the interviewer that upsetting the "corporate culture is our one great fear".

Since the overriding result of Office Systems Technology is to create a massive culture change, that's one dread that will have to be exorcised by all managements wanting to participate in the office revolution as it is made. The case which Zuboff refers to as "Global Bank Brazil" illustrates the point precisely. This was the only service organisation she studied that was attempting to grasp hold of the new office technology in order to accomplish major strategic change – an effort which, by the time she finished her studies, was incomplete.

She learnt enough, however, to observe that "As time-frames become more immediate, as more sectors of data can be integrated, as software helps limit inaccuracies, as data entry and access become more widely distributed, and as programmed logic becomes more comprehensible and flexible, the surrounding life-world of the organisation comes to be more comprehensively reflected in a dynamic, fluid electronic text."

What this means, in bald terms, is that routine, structured work becomes more and more mechanical (or electronic); still newer technology (like "sophisticated automated data-entry devices based on optical character recognition") will further reduce the people and the intellectual effort required for routine transactions executed via the machine system. The system, however, doesn't stop at its own boundaries. It provides the material and means for more effective thinking in ways that are "conceptual, inferational, procedural and systemic".

Zuboff concludes that exploiting these powers (human powers potentiated and exercised through the system) runs up against "realities that cut to the quick of managerial power as it is conceived and displayed in everyday life at work". She is referring here to internal realities. But external realities ultimately have the decisive power: and those of the competitive marketplace, as much as the realities of the rising office generation, mean that the race will go to the quick – and those who cut to the quick.

Chapter 18

THE STRATEGY OF INFORMATION

If any one technological advance brings home to senior managers the range and depth of the office revolution it will be executive information: the ability to conjure forth, in their own offices, or on their laps, detailed facts, without the intervention of any assistants of any grade, that will lead directly to profitable management decisions. If that sounds like the Holy Grail of management, sought in vain down the ages, an account in *Fortune* magazine, dated 13th March, 1989, tells the truth: tomorrow's dream is today's reality.

The article, by Jeremy Main, tells the tale of Robert Kidder, chief executive officer of Duracell, and one of the users of the company's executive information system. Mouse in hand, Kidder spent an hour at his workstation, using his personal computer to search through the banks of data in the corporate mainframe. He wanted information "comparing the performance of the Duracell hourly and salaried work forces in the UK and overseas. Within seconds the computer produced a crisp, clear table in colours showing that the US salaried staff produced more sales per employee."

That fact in itself raised questions, but provided no answers. The computer did. Investigating further, Kidder discovered that salespeople in West Germany were devoting unproductive time to visits to small stockists of the company's alkaline batteries. "The information helped explain profit problems there. As a result Duracell cut the German sales staff and signed up distributors to cover the mom and pop stores."

The issue isn't that chief executives, or other senior managers, can't find such information from the traditional office. But the internal memo and the squawk box are no match in immediacy, speed, completeness and productivity for the computerised executive information system, or EIS. Even in its infancy, EIS holds out the prospect of immediate gains as well as long-term advances of sweeping

129

importance. "The system has been useful," Kidder told Main, "and we are a long way from getting the most out of it."

As so often, the story is of separate technologies advancing along a convergent path. Main points out that PCs had to become powerful enough to convert the mass of stored data into highly readable tables and charts; devices replacing the keyboard – the touch screen and the mouse – gave swifter and easier to learn communication with the computer; software tied the electronic capabilities together into a system with which men like Kidder could feel comfortable – and familiarity then turned the comfort into necessity.

Paul Lego, the chairman of Westinghouse, puts the initial gains in a nutshell. "This hasn't completely changed the way I manage, but I feel a lot more comfortable with the decisions I have made." The certainty, however, is that the way in which chief executives manage, and in which their offices are run, will change completely as a result of EIS and other advances in the management of information. This was clearly recognised by Paul Allaire, president of Xerox Corporation: in his company reporting, planning and the organisation of meetings have all been changed in response to the rise in electronic capability.

By the time these words are read, the market for packaged information systems will probably have doubled. In 1988, according to International Data, it rose by 45% to $32 million, but this is plainly only the tip of the iceberg. Throw in custom-built systems, and the number of companies using EIS will surely be in four figures – and interest is clearly burgeoning. In 1988, a British conference organiser had to move a seminar on EIS when several hundred companies sought places, instead of the dozens originally expected.

Demonstration of a screen-based information system is guaranteed to make easy converts. In a typical package, Comshare's Commander, the user is offered a choice of four displays: "briefing book", "Execuview", "Newswire" and "Redi-Mail". Choosing "briefing book", he gets a choice of six screens: "financial performance", "markets and products", "customers", "human resources", "production" and "planning and people". He calls up "financial performance", which shows divisional sales in July, with the fall in one division's sales picked out in red. To investigate this discrepancy, the boss can call up a bar chart showing the year's trends, analyse the truant division's sales by type, and finally isolate the cause of the sale decline.

It sounds like a fascinating game – and future generations of executives, brought up on TV games as children, will find these manipulations to be child's play. But the results are deadly serious, especially for the layers of middle managers whose employment has been largely as executive postboxes (Peter Drucker's "relays"), receiving queries from above and raising answers from below. The human postboxes not only get in the way of speedy and effective decision and implementation: they use office space and salaries to little real purpose, and are often inefficient.

Either the information can't be found, or it is coloured by personal prejudices and vested interests, or it gets distorted – as in the game of "Chinese whispers", when a message whispered at one end of the line comes out as something completely different at the other. The advantage of the EIS applies to both passive and active data. Passive data refers to information like the names and telephone numbers of the managers running a particular operation; active data means, say, discovering which version of a product has been selling most strongly in which type of outlet – from which policy decisions may well flow.

The consequences for the office are obvious: fewer executives and secretaries, less paper, less time wasted in chasing data. But the consequences for management, and thus again for the office, run far deeper. Allaire's changes at Xerox were a state-of-the-art example in the eighties, and, like all such developments, the blueprint for run-of-the-mill systems of the nineties. *Fortune* called the "executive support system" devised by Allaire "probably the most far-reaching in any company" and one that "goes to the heart of management".

You can see why from this description of what used to go on before and during the annual meetings between the top executives at headquarters and the heads of the twenty strategic business units at Xerox. Writes Main, "Torrents of paper would rush back and forth in the preceding few days. Senior executives would get a fat black briefing book of documents, only partly read and little digested before the meeting, with no consistent format or terminology. Two similar units might have different definitions of a basic term like revenue. Much of a meeting would be spent trying to agree on facts."

The picture is depressingly familiar to anybody who attends most board meetings, even in companies far smaller than Xerox. The new system, for a start, eliminates the paperwork. Five days before the meeting, a five-page electronic plan, using standard definitions of terms, is submitted to headquarters. Before the executives gather at Stamford, Connecticut, the top management will have read all twenty plans seated at their Xerox 6085 work stations. With the facts no longer in dispute, the issues can be disputed.

The Xerox system has become the subject of a Harvard Business School case study in which Allaire says that "our management process is becoming inseparable from the technology which supports it" – a statement that will obviously become still more emphatic as the Xerox system, first confined to fifteen top executives, then extended to 100, spreads down the ranks, perhaps to as many as 500 managers.

Some of the benefits are obvious and non-controversial – like speeding up the monthly figures by several days. If the evidence of consultants United Research is correct, EIS quadruples the time spent in meetings on real management issues, reversing the traditional proportions. Where "sharing information and just trying to agree on facts" could take 80% of a typical business meeting, with only 20% spent on "planning, solving problems and making decisions", the latter can now occupy 80% of the time.

That, too, sounds like a non-controversial benefit. But the 80% figure correlates ominously with another four-fifths: to quote Main, "a middle manager spends 80% of his time collecting, analysing, and passing on information. He might be spooked by knowing the chairman or president can probe into his work without leaving a trace." That fear can be dealt with automatically: at Xerox, Main reports, there are limits to how far the support system will "drill down". The computer will provide corporate, major business unit and subdivision figures, but at that third layer it stops.

The fear of the boss looking over your shoulder, however, is far less dreadful than that of having no boss – and no job either. If four-fifths of a middle manager's time is spent acting as an information postbox, the elimination of that task suggests, on the face of it, that only a fifth of existing middle management will be required in the revolutionised office. Consciously or subconsciously, many middle managers are well aware of the threat, which could act as a major restraint on the progress of the revolution.

David De Long of the Harvard Business School, who has written a book (*Executive Support Systems*) on the subject with John Rockart of MIT, says that "You should anticipate organisational resistance, because an executive information system is inherently political. After all, you are changing information flows and access. That's very threatening." But the resistance can't do more than delay the revolution, because the benefits are simply too great – and because the revolution can easily be imposed from the top.

In this, the leaders will be aided, abetted and spurred on by the grey eminences who go under names like "director of information systems". The latter have learnt that an effective EIS can only arise from decisions taken by the top executives themselves: only they know what information they require. The job of the information specialists is to provide what Rockart calls "critical success factors" – data ranging from current sales (in one example he quotes) through sales of technically advanced products to how customers perceived the quality of the company's engineers.

There's a passage by Sir John Harvey-Jones, in his excellent book, *Making It Happen*, that illuminates the process. Shortly after the start of his chairmanship at ICI:

> we obtained a very fine piece of equipment, which enabled us to "interact" with the financial data presented to us. We had formerly received this as a book, in tabular form, which involved very large amounts of work by each of us to try to discern the trends which lay behind the tables. Thanks to modern technology, and some splendid support work by a number of our people, it became possible for us to sit in front of a screen and, for the first time, see the development of the trends in the individual businesses and economies in which we were interested, and also to indulge in a certain number of "what if" questions on the run.

Harvey-Jones notes that an astonishing transformation took place. "We found to our surprise that suddenly the whole of our business became alive to us all. We were all joining the discussion, forming our judgments and views and were able to express concerns that we had about the business in a lively way." Not only did this prove to be "a very useful board tool", but (again "to our surprise") the fact that the board was working with its computerised system in this way began to filter back down the organisation. Replicas began to appear, "albeit in different and more adventurous ways".

From this process, set up "without any dark intent", the board and "a number of our businesses began looking at the database in similar interactive ways, and learning from each other". Harvey-Jones calls this a "very good example of a situation where a matter of selection of style had effects far beyond those which were originally intended". That process is being repeated now, and will be repeated generally, in company after company. Once a board and its individual members get accustomed to seeing critical information and trends highlighted in colour, their style of management changes accordingly, and so does that of their reporting executives.

Robert Wallace, the retired president of Phillips Petroleum's refining and marketing side, echoed Harvey-Jones when he talked to *Fortune*: "I can see trends in seconds. I can't do that if I'm scanning a lot of tables on paper." He cites as an example of the benefits the ability to monitor price trends while leaving the actual fixing to local managements – with results that Wallace estimates improved oil trading profits by two-thirds to $50 million a year. Given that the cost for a packaged system in 1989 ran from $100,000 to $280,000 for ten stations, with an additional $1,500 per station and 15% maintenance charge, that has to be a bargain.

But the costs will assuredly come down as the technical possibilities go up. The day is coming when a company-wide EIS will be no costlier than an executive work station at 1989 prices, and even more convenient to use than the present packages. Sound and video recording capabilities are fast on the way, along with remote control facilities, to replace the mouse and the touchscreen. The lap-top is already here: the EIS can be loaded onto the hard disc and updated by phone from anywhere in the world. And, to repeat Harvey-Jones's eloquent phrase, the whole of the business will still come alive – on the lap, or anywhere else the executive wants. Not only has the office become mobile: so has the whole company.

Chapter 19

THE RESPONSE OF RANK XEROX

In the first chapter of this book, I described visiting the still-unoccupied bank and being seized by its resemblance – despite the banks of computer terminals and the immaculate work station furniture – to the bullpen insurance office that Jack Lemmon inhabited, with hundreds of other clerks, at the start of *The Apartment*.

This, I knew, wasn't the office of the future, but the last incarnation of the office of the past. The present, let alone the future, lies rather in the wide open spaces of the executive floor of Rank Xerox (UK) in Uxbridge. Here, too, every desk had a terminal. But these were linked, not only to each other, but to mainframe and minicomputers throughout the Xerox Corporation world. One of the executives, in another set of offices, dominated by state-of-the-art equipment, had shown how, in seconds, he could check the appointments schedule of a colleague on the West Coast of the United States, draw on the same file that the colleague had been using, send him back-and-forth messages: all without budging from his British desk.

All these transactions, moreover, took place on an unusually large screen, a "window" covered with "icons" – symbols for the files and programs being employed. The Rank Xerox offices also sported easels and flipcharts, covered with large scribbles. In this office culture the graphic representation of ideas had become the norm. The Xerox Corporation research laboratories at Palo Alto had developed the mouse, icon and window concepts on the well-known theory that symbolic representation increases the power of communication; the computer screen itself, a graphic version of an ordinary desk-top, incorporates the same idea.

It was a brilliant intuition, which is undoubtedly becoming the basis of the easy-to-use computers of the future. Lack of ease in use, or user-hostility, has probably been the main reason why managements have lagged behind yesterday's revolutionary developments in the office, let alone today's or tomorrow's. Rank Xerox, I knew, had been fighting an uphill struggle to interest its customers – who include virtually every major company in Britain – in the new office: even though its own experience, and its success in turning round its own traditional British business in copiers, demonstrated that this pie was not in the sky.

The company's office strategy rested on six simple pillars which will already be familiar from earlier chapters:

1. Automation has to relate to what actually happens in offices.
2. A human, easily recognised and used interface with the technology is essential.
3. The architecture of the system must be based on document management, which is the basis of office work.
4. Document management must be integrated with the architecture of the system managing the corporate database.
5. The system must be comprehensively networked.
6. It must lay the foundation for building in applications of artificial intelligence as these develop.

The most obvious feature in the Uxbridge offices is the first result of this strategy: the integrated work station with its graphic displays that translate exactly into output ("what you see is what you get") from the imitation of a working desktop; hardware that is operated, not through learned combinations of numbers and letters, but through the visible, self-explanatory devices of the icons, windows, pull-down menus and pop-up property sheets; screen contents that are all actuated easily by the pointer on the screen, controlled by the little switching device (the mouse) on the desk.

The workstations are linked through the cabling to facilities for electronic printing and publishing, and with each other, by an Ethernet local area network and with other Xerox offices by inter-networking: Xerox Network Services handles both. The system is cogent, coherent and competent. It's hard to believe that even keyboard-shy managers, shown theory turned into efficient practice, could ignore the evidence of their own eyes – yet the slow take-up of Office Systems Technology can't be ignored, either. Plainly, in the late eighties the concept couldn't be sold in terms of straight benefits, like a mobile phone: "You can ring the office from anywhere, and be rung ... I'll have one." Plainly, "you can be in continuous contact with your entire business", while a vastly more powerful concept, has run into roadblocks in all too many companies.

There is a major philosophical barrier. The starting point for the strategy of Office Systems Technology is that successful installation requires matching it to the true office requirement – which is reflected in very few current environments. The change is far-reaching: both the change and its costs are system-wide. It's as if buying that mobile phone meant purchasing, not stand-alone devices, but a whole new system and concept of telecommunications. For a manager who isn't used to thinking of his business or his office as a system, that requires a major jump into a future where the actual payoffs can seem somewhat vague.

There are none so blind, of course, as those who will not see. The Rank Xerox managers themselves have seen. They have come to think in terms of the "management process", broken down by functions, and operating through the divisional structure to achieve sets of objectives from which roles and responsibilities can be derived. In their minds, and in their electronic office, this forms a complete system, within which answers to problems can be sought by pulling all relevant information together on the screen and the flipcharts.

The screen will, for instance, summon up the "business environment" in a grid that neatly combines the "business areas" (financial management and reporting, installed equipment management, etc.) and the "roles and responsibilities" (marketing, personnel, etc.) along the route from the "source of supply" to "the market". To give a practical example, it was within this "quantification" of the 1989 Business Plan that the executives set about manpower rationalisation: with the numbers of indirect manpower a particular issue.

They started with two assumptions: that in parts, or "processes" of the business which were relatively mature and "non-strategic" (i.e. focused internally, not externally), there were very probably too many people. In the relatively immature and strategic (i.e. customer-focused) areas, the reverse was most likely to be true. From these two assumptions followed three conclusions. They needed to identify the company's business processes according to their strategic and maturity status; to target the non-strategic mature areas where activities could be eliminated; and, by the opposite token, to target the strategic, immature processes where greater resources in levels of skill, numbers and technology could be profitably applied.

The computer turned this thinking into a matrix. "Strategic" was defined as "supporting tomorrow's customer, supporting the business mission and agreed business priorities" – the latter being customer satisfaction, market share and return on assets. Mid-way between the extremes of strategy and non-strategy lay activities "essential in maintaining the company's infrastructure". "Non-strategic" was simply defined: "those things we choose to do". The "mature" was "well-established, well understood", with "in-depth experience"; the "immature", in contrast, was "not robust, not understood", and demanded "rare expertise".

Very rapidly, the business processes were analysed along these lines, and the computer displayed the results by function: 64 strategic processes, 83 non-strategic. For instance, 19 out of the 22 customer support processes were strategic, against three out of the 23 in asset management. The analysis led to the second phase of the rationalisation review. Again there were two assumptions: that "indirect staff do not create business transactions – their role is analysis, co-ordination, communication"; and, thus, the resources needed had to be "directly proportional to (1) the frequency (2) the quality required in the analysis and communication".

The conclusion was to "review activities in non-strategic/mature processes" by frequency and quality, so that those with the lowest frequency and quality needs could be targeted for elimination. Another matrix was constructed, dividing 576 activities by frequency (as compared to infrequency) and "personnel consumption" (against "customer consumption"). This further digging down the organisation enabled Phase Three of the rationalisation to proceed. Its assumptions were that *all* indirect (analysis and communication) activities could potentially be eliminated by one or a combination of methods:

1. Cost displacement
(a) application of technology – to quality and frequency requirements;
(b) subcontracting of *direct* activities (which would remove the need for analysis and communication).
2. Changes in roles and responsibilities – by cross-functional integration.
3. Simplifying processes – by removing steps in the process.
4. Process facilitation – using Office Systems Technology itself.
5. Functional reorganisation – combining jobs where activities have been eliminated.
6. Increasing spans of control.

The process of reducing numbers then swiftly continued – 142 of the people employed in the lowest-scoring business processes and activities were surplus to requirement in those jobs. The how and when of the savings, like all the analysis that preceded them, were established within the system – which enabled the policy committee at all times to operate within a full overview of the business and with full information immediately available from the data which the system held.

This exercise was essentially negative (but highly positive financially); while it was going on, however, the wholly positive side of the rationalisation was also proceeding – Phase Four, the review of strategic and immature processes. Once again, this required review of activities on the matrix of frequency and quality. Once again, this required targets and priorities: but this time for additions to resources, not subtraction.

The assumptions for Phase Five were that the three-year business plans would supply the direction for strategic developments. They would be achieved by adding:

1. Skill – by training.
2. Numbers of people.
3. Technology.
4. Cash.
5. Other arrangements.

The conclusion was that the extra resources had to be identified within each business plan. Added to the identified cutbacks in non-strategic areas, this would complete the rationalisation. That resulted, as it happens, in a plan to cut numbers from 1,187 at the end of the 1988 financial year to 1,098 in 1989 and 1,021 a year after that – all against a background of vigorous expansion in sales and activity to promote future growth.

This exercise, at one level, illustrates how Office Systems Technology enables management to conduct detailed, action-oriented studies within a logical, policy-driven framework without needing many man-hours of supplemental staff work. At a higher level, though, the rationalisation plan is a single example of how the technology facilitates what the company calls the "team management process". Itself embroiled in one of the world's most competitive marketplaces, where Japanese industry meets the West head-on, Rank Xerox had to respond to the external forces for which its product and marketing strategy was designed.

The physician had to heal himself – before being able to offer the same treatment to its customers. The response could not consist of technology alone. The crux of the office revolution is that culture, or corporate philosophy, must be revolutionised as well. To exploit the potential of information technology for itself and its customers, the management had to lead the cultural revolution, which goes beyond hardware and software technology into the changed working relationships and attitudes that new technology enables.

It's possible to detect a note of frustration among the managers in the front line of the revolution at the difficulty of conveying its full significance to a stubborn outside world. Like riding a bicycle, to take a homely example, it cannot be explained easily to somebody who has never tried it – or even seen a bike. The collective, post-revolutionary managerial mind gets habituated to charts and diagrams, to thinking graphically about problems and solutions in ways that the computer facilitates and reinforces. The unaccustomed mind looks at the graphics and can't relate them to the business data which, in such a system, are the fuel and raw material of decision support.

Team management "to implement change" is symbolised to the Rank Xerox executives by three pyramids, each in three sections. The first consists, from apex to base, of roles and responsibilities, business processes, and activities. Again from top to bottom, these elements are changed by business development planning, business systems requirements, and quality improvement. They lead to the middle pyramid: from apex to base, they are business priorities, strategic value/maturity analysis, and frequency/quality analysis. From here the final pyramid can be constructed: revised roles and responsibilities at the top; then changed business processes; then restructured essential activities.

Put like that, and portrayed like that, it all sounds quite simple. The essence of the new world into which management is moving – much faster than it knows – is to use extreme sophistication of technology to simplify the process of management. What you can actually see happening graphically before your eyes is much easier to grasp than abstract conceptual thought. What you see is what you get in more senses than one. When business itself is getting more complex on every dimension, the simplification of the management process – while intensifying the power of thought and the intelligence of applied information – is the only intelligent response. The intelligent system breeds intelligent management. Its opposite can only have opposite results.

Chapter 20

THE POWERS OF OST

Office Systems Technology won't deliver all its benefits at a single blow, like the purchase of the first typewriter. Even with those primitive forerunners of today's complex and sophisticated machines, use and experience extended the potential of the machine and increased its productivity. But a dynamic, interactive office system, binding together hardware, software and people in new and untried combinations, is bound to develop and grow as it goes along.

Only when office users have begun to discover the utility of new facilities, like the "browse and discover" search through files and directories, will they become addicted to this invaluable extension of their powers of reference and cross-reference. Only when they have begun to use the system to exchange views and opinions, and to modify positions as a result of the interchange, will this collegiate aspect of the office become second managerial nature.

But there is a new world that goes beyond these horizons. The computer can examine relationships and do a logical check for matches and coherence: it can, in other words, learn the rules and ensure that they are being applied. Its formidable powers in this respect have made it unbeatable at draughts, and only vulnerable to the very greatest players at chess. But you don't win at chess by obeying the rules. You also need to *know* an enormous amount about the game, and to be able to *predict* the outcome of moves far ahead.

OST will provide the first half of the last sentence: an enormous amount of information, or knowledge. But how can this wealth of knowledge be applied to achieve winning management? The analogy of the chess-playing computer suggests the answer. The system can learn rules, assimilate knowledge and combine the two to draw conclusions. It can, in other words, become artificially intelligent, systematically expert. Many expert systems are now in use – some of them are already veterans. Most uses have not particularly helped management to manage in the widest sense: but they have made distinctly useful contributions to business results – and to greater office efficiency.

For example, American Express has an expert system which checks in seconds whether an unusually large purchase should be authorised for a particular customer. The company claims that an assistant's productivity has risen by up to 20%, while losses from ill-judged authorisations have fallen. Digital Equipment has a now famous system called XCON, started as long ago as 1973, which analyses every order, works out the right configuration of components, and has enabled the company to save, not only much manual work, but $25 million from reducing the amount of final assembly required at the plant.

An expert on artificial intelligence, Beau Sheil, has commented (*Harvard Business Review*, July/August 1987) that XCON is one of the "low-responsibility applications in which the consequences of errors are nil" to which artificial intelligence, in its then state of development, could be safely applied. Sheil notes that "The occasional mistake can be rectified easily by an extra shipment of parts. The hitch, of course, is that most routine decision problems of this type can be solved with much simpler, less intelligent technology."

Sheil, whose background includes both the Palo Alto Research Center and the Artificial Intelligence Systems Unit of Xerox Corporation, has some other highly intelligent observations about AI – considerations which will plainly govern its development. But before summarising these sometimes cautionary views, it's advisable to take an incautious view of the prospect. Within a relatively short timespan, professionals in virtually all offices will be using expert systems of one kind or another as a routine part of the operations – with no more hesitancy or difficulty than they now show with a pocket calculator.

The calculator is a good analogy. Everybody using one can add, subtract, multiply and divide by hand or mind. But the electronic device does so more rapidly, and infallibly at that. In exactly the same way, asked to price an order, a salesman can type in the relevant details, and the expert system will tell him the permissible price range. Or a maintenance engineer calls to check a defective piece of equipment. He keys in the results of his check, and the expert system says what is probably wrong, and what will probably cure the defect.

Note the "probably". Human "experts" are not infallible, and there's no reason to expect electronic experts to escape fallibility – especially since the construction of the systems will depend on human expertise in the first place. But the expert systems will be more consistent than human beings and more consistently thorough – that is, they are incapable of ignoring any rule, or failing to check any possibility, that has once been brought to their attention.

The systems are therefore more reliably accurate. In any situation where formal rules, "rules of thumb" and know-how can be codified (and that applies to most management and office activities), expert systems will be the first port of call – resorted to by the managing director as automatically as he turns to the financial director with a query about the management of the group's cash balances.

The financial director is, of course, a highly trained specialist, and Sheil makes the point that "it will be easier to build systems for highly specialised problems than for broad, general ones, since the amount of knowledge required for a narrow problem is typically much smaller." He is against Manhattan Project-type approaches – a Big Bang effort to create a huge breakthrough in automated decision-making. He is for precisely the kind of uses mentioned above: "to package AI technology as an 'assistant to' rather than as the primary decision-maker".

Human assistants, he argues, "have some knowledge, they help, but are expected to make occasional mistakes, and they assist a person who bears the responsibility for any mistakes". It doesn't take much thought to see that the "assistant to" or servant role has potential that goes well beyond that of the masterful, comprehensive, omniscient machine. Even if the latter could be built, would it be obeyed? As Sheil asks, if a medical diagnostician could be entirely replaced by an expert system, which is probably not feasible, or an airline crew by artificial intelligence (AI), which is perfectly feasible, who would risk their lives in either case on the word of a machine?

The technological task of producing brilliant assistants is not lower-order. But Sheil points out that AI applications are especially well suited to "exploratory programming", in which the designer doesn't really know where he's going until he gets there. That idea fits in well with developments in British practice as outlined by Alex d'Agapayeff in *Management 90*. In contrast to the "American tradition of large-scale applications that were expensive, risky and demanding but could (and in Digital's case did) produce high returns", the British have preferred a quite different tradition: smaller, low-cost and less risky, with "initially modest but gradually increasing benefits".

The British companies, says d'Agapayeff, "built computer programs from the explicit know-how, or rules of thumb, of different experts, so that this professional expertise could be studied and exploited by intended users *in a way that suited these users best*". Note the last eight, italicised words. D'Agapayeff's own company, Expertech, produces software that has now resulted in 200 business applications – "by far the most popular structure" is used to clarify regulations, with tasks ranging from staff mortgages to clearing up spills of toxic chemicals.

The so-called British approach suggests an analogy with the development of computing itself. Like expert systems, computers began big – and expensive. Then, as power increased and size diminished, the machines became small and relatively very cheap. At the same time, the nature and expense of software moved in the same direction – large-scale, custom-tailored programs were succeeded, and in some cases superseded, by thousands of editioned software packages, sold in the same manner as paperback books.

The analogy goes further. In the wondrous saga of the personal computer, there was a major element of do-it-yourself. Not only were the first PCs imported into business use by free-thinking managers, but the initial growth took place entirely outside the mainstream hardware and software companies. A great deal of improvisation took place, too, as PC enthusiasts discovered their powers of experimentation – and a pair of expert systems experts, Dorothy Leonard-Barton and John V. Sviokla, suggest that this experimental approach can be built into a corporate policy.

The technique is that of "making PC-based skills widely available to end-users. The idea is that, as people become comfortable with the technology, they will discover useful applications on their own." Writing in the *Harvard Business Review* (March–April 1988), the two authors gave the example of Du Pont. Employees were provided with expert system skills and encouraged "to build systems tailored to their specific needs". The payback and the development time for these small projects are both expected to be quick.

The idea of producing your own expert system may sound far beyond the powers of the typical manager, or even most untypical ones. But the word "expert", like the phrase "artificial intelligence", is misleading in this context. These systems are not intended to mimic or surpass the brain of the normal human being, let alone the expert. They should really be called "know-how systems". D'Agapayeff describes know-how as "the product of experience in doing a job which determines the overwhelming majority of decisions taken by veterans in carrying out that job".

He notes that these rules of thumb vary from expert to expert. But "similar experience does give rise to similar rules" – and it is these which the assembled experts bring together when working on a system. As with all automation, the very act of working through the unautomated process has great benefits in itself. But the end-result is that companies are already gaining from:

144

1. Clarifying regulations.
2. Fault diagnosis.
3. Training.
4. Advanced applications.

D'Agapayeff lists, under the last heading, alarm condition handling, financial risk analysis, advising customers and decision support systems – noting that these "are normally closely tied into specific business contexts and are rarely described publicly". One less esoteric advanced business use, though, is the management information system. For example, technical or marketing managers may not get the enlightenment they want from regular accounting-based reports: "In reality, managers have to balance a mix of priorities and goals, some of which may conflict, and few are measured by accountancy." In such cases, as he says, there's an apparent better strategy: "a front-end expert system linked to databases and other files that enables a manager to browse through particular information assembled according to his requests".

The manager himself would be "the expert", feeding in the know-how about the market or the technical performance data that signal meaningful variances and changes. This example shows how these new "experts" will make their marks – by making generally available what is currently only known to individual experts. This has the far from incidental benefit that know-how won't leave the company with its possessor. The acquired know-how of the past will be available to everybody in the present – and in a future when the powers of expert systems and artificial intelligence may well exceed the bounds of current imagination.

Quite apart from technological achievements still to come, there's the cumulative effect of expert systems as both training and operating tool. A system that takes staff through the procedures of dealing with a customer teaches as it assists; so does a system that helps a young manager to complete a business plan. Interactive and adaptable, the expert systems promise to make both office and management processes swifter and less prone to obvious error. These are important gains, and they don't come up against Beau Sheil's barrier.

"The fundamental issues for operational deployment," he wrote, "are predictability and acceptability" – which you won't find typically in an AI system that "makes guesses". But "even if predictable competence were not an issue, wouldn't any manager still hesitate before making intelligent systems responsible for major business decisions?" The Sheil barrier is a real one. But the constraint doesn't limit the huge potential growth. Ever since John Seely Brown of Xerox's Palo

Alto Research Center pointed out that AI software technology had what Sheil calls an "enabling role" to play in helping to produce conventional applications more rapidly, the utility of AI has been proving and expanding itself.

Already simple "rule interpreters" like those mentioned by d'Agapayeff are helping practical business people on employment legislation, security procedures when auditing specific types of computer system, and compliance with complex financial regulations. As Sheil writes, "the sceptic might ask how much real intelligence there is" in deciding "which sales forms to send a customer or what details of the tax code to represent". But, of course, there wasn't much intelligence involved when humans did the same job unaided. The systems will free the human brain for the unstructured tasks which it does best – in and out of the office.

Expert systems will consolidate the power of Office Systems Technology to improve the effectiveness of the unstructured roles. The key is to employ technology that specifically supports these activities. Where office automation has applied technology to discrete activities, "office systems" applies it to the support of overall processes in the office. Expert systems and AI create the final, vital difference between, on the one hand, applying technology to order entry, input to computer systems, simple text editing, etc., and, on the other hand, achieving integration and successful use of the technology. With that achieved, the system can support, not just a few activities, but the vital processes in the office – right up to the creation of ideas.

BOOK V
The Shape of Things to Come

Chapter 21

THE PHASES OF TECHNOLOGY

In the beginning, there was the crunching of numbers. In the fifties and sixties, the notion that the evolution of the computer would lead to a revolution in the office couldn't even be dimly glimpsed. Extravagant claims were made about the abilities of these amazing machines even then. But in hard reality, computers were mostly used to enable companies to achieve tasks – most of them routine – that were simply not practical on a manual basis.

The less managements expected from the computer installations, the less likely they were to be disappointed. Users were driven by the computational capacity of the machines, and very quickly saw the need (and the technical capability) to automate some functions. In the second generation of the computer era, this functionality became dominant. Clear operational requirements emerged which could again be met – and often only be met – by the emerging technology.

People began to cost-justify applications. It was no longer a question of "Here is a computational problem – how do we solve it?" Now an operational need could be identified and a transaction-processing solution could be applied. Systems for airline and other reservations were for many people, on both sides of the counter, their first introduction to the screen as the eyes and ears of the computer and, at the same time, an extension of the powers of its remote operators.

Phrases like "real-time" and "on-line" expressed the reality of live interaction between the user and the machine. Computing had moved from historic data to current data. But in its prolonged adolescence, the computing age built up a legacy of misunderstanding and mistrust which may in part explain why, in the relative maturity of four decades and $222 billion of cumulative business, people are readier to repeat the myths than to realise the benefits of the Third Age of the computer – the Age of Information.

Unisys, the corporation formed out of Sperry Univac (the first computer company) and Burroughs, has usefully listed the myths which still prevailed in 1989:

1. Computers are meant for number-crunching.
2. Companies will never agree on standards.
3. Building multi-vendor networks is a nightmare.
4. It's easier to change your business than your software.

The myths faithfully reflect the growing up of the industry, starting with the crunching of numbers. That is still basic work, ranging from payroll, money-processing and scores of other humdrum necessities up to vast statistical efforts which, in human terms, are equally dull but on which some of the world's most dramatic technological advances are founded.

As the technology has developed, so the costs have come down – that of mainframe computing has fallen by some 20% a year for the past twenty years. As size has fallen along with price, speed has improved to a colossal extent. Planning has been unable to cope with the results. I once visited a Science Park near Nice where only Air France had been allowed to build above the regulation two storeys. The park desperately needed the airline, and the airline desperately needed – or so its management thought – enough space to accommodate its future computer requirements. By the time of my visit, the computer installation occupied only a part of a single floor.

There's a parallel here with the office developments of the Age of Information. The skyscrapers have been rising higher and higher to provide room for larger and larger armies of office workers who may simply not be needed – not in these central locations, at any rate. The computer centre itself, for a start, is shrinking even as computerisation becomes crucial to the life of every part of the organisation. The backroom boys who controlled, and alone understood, the workings of the computer and its programs, are vestiges of the past. That past has retreated with the advance of powerful computing capacity from the sealed-off "clean room" to the hurly-burly of the open office and the executive desk.

In the new modes, computers tend to reduce needs for highly skilled staff, not increase them. Unisys lists three areas where, by going beyond cost-cutting and speedier transaction processing, information systems can automate work that would otherwise require the efforts of many high-calibre staff:

The Phases of Technology

1. Anticipation of, and reaction to, changing market trends.
2. Analysis of the effectiveness of services, products and business strategies.
3. Reduction of inventories by forecasting product sales and matching material orders and output rates to the forecasts.

The advance of computers into these zones has, in effect, meant automating management decisions. What's happening in the market, and what should we do about it? How well is that service, that product, that strategy, actually working out? Should we be raising or cutting the rate of output? Yet the full benefit of these managerial powers couldn't be obtained for what seems, in hindsight, an absurd reason. Computers couldn't talk to, or work with, one another – entirely because each supplier, seeking to bind its customers exclusively to itself, maintained its own, separate exclusive system.

To quote Unisys again, "What resulted was the computer industry's version of the Tower of Babel. Machines couldn't communicate, and software applications couldn't be moved from one type of system to another. Customers stayed with the same vendor to ensure that at least some of the systems worked together." The Tower of Babel is now being pulled down – partly by the suppliers, who have banded together, often under user pressure, to achieve agreement on "open systems" of various kinds; partly by the technologists, who have solved many of the tricky problems of getting different computers to speak the same language.

In 1989, every computer supplier, from mainframes to minis, was committed to alliances that would make the complete corporate system possible, and with it the transformation of the office. That commitment means that, in a future that is almost upon the industry as I write, users will take it for granted that their information systems, whether bought from one supplier or many, will be totally cohesive. That, in turn, will exploit the powers of networks to the full – and networking is the key to the third computer age.

All the above discussion, though, stops short of the change which truly marks the advent of the new age. Unisys mentions a fourth function of the modern information system, "to give decision-makers the information they need, when and where they need it". It's hard to argue with the company's injunction: "Information is your key productive resource. Use it strategically and profit. Ignore it and fail." But how can that injunction be obeyed most effectively?

Today's generation of computer development has seen the strategic value of information become apparent, though not yet dominant, not because new technologies have yet to arise – they have arisen in impressive panoply – but because the awareness of managers, above all senior managers, has not yet crossed the threshold of the new age. Database systems have been created to handle data in ways that, for the first time, have made it possible to build up the management of information.

Decision support systems live up to the name: their users can get access to the information in the database and improve the ways in which the data is deployed – by themselves, without the necessary intervention of the high priests of the computer. The third age has taken management into the heart of office automation, where the gains have been immediate and self-evident. No longer do computer sales people have to hold out vague promises of future gold. The information nuggets can be mined right now – in today's real time.

Time, in the sense of seizing the opportunities, has passed many managements by. As long ago as the autumn of 1987, William J. Bruns Jr and F. Warren McFarlan reported on impressive examples of new technology applied to strategic ends.

... An insurance company reorganised its computer files by customer instead of policy number. The old system, listing customer names in various different ways, made it all but impossible for sales people to discover the full range of insurance products purchased by each customer. This encouraged the pursuit of short-term sales and discouraged the creation of long-term relationships with customers. So did the commission system. After the expensive reorganisation of the files, the commission system could be reversed – and, able to review a customer's entire insurance picture, the sales side could "use this information for suggesting replacement of outdated insurance or other financial instrument holdings".

... A company making passenger lifts centralised a decentralised service system. Beforehand, customer calls for service were handled at branch offices and reported to head office only in summary form – through four reporting levels, which greatly reduced the chances of top management learning about causes of complaint. The creation of "a massive centralised database" enabled the company to (a) identify problem areas, involving product design or staff performance, (b) improve servicing by giving the service people a full history of each elevator.

... Supermarket chains all over the world no longer have to rely on employees to count stock as the basis for buying and purchasing. The data were often too late to prevent over-stocking, or out-of-stock, for that matter. Electronic point of sale has totally changed the dynamics of store operations: the stock count is continuous, is

accurate and is linked to instantaneous analysis of stock requirements. Inventory levels have fallen, and what the authors describe
as the "speed and flexibility" of these new systems have made store
operations faster and more flexible in turn.

Bruns and McFarlan, however, were writing in the context of
control systems. As they write:

> Managers once stymied by the languorous flow of information from
> the workforce or from customers can now grab data from the most
> remote corners of their companies in an instant. Key facts – from
> the slowing inventory turnover of an offshore plant to the sudden
> burst of sales in a distant territory – that were previously filtered
> out or obscured can now be presented in whatever form makes
> decision-making easiest. . . . Those that selected wisely from the
> new list of options have seen their control systems and structures
> transformed . . . they have boosted their efficiency and overall com-
> petitive position.

All that is perfectly true. The companies described have indeed
"found ways to channel the power of information to the muscles
of their corporations". Within two years of that article appearing,
however, the office revolution had moved on to a whole new plane.
The issue had become how to channel information, not to the muscles
of the corporation, but to its mind. With each generation of computer
development, the systems in use have been governed by the architectural base of the system itself and very much geared to the structured
activities – which is evidently true of the three cases mentioned above.
  If the efficiency of the office and the effectiveness of management
are to be revolutionised, as this book has stressed, the demands of
unstructured activities must be equally well understood, equally well
integrated into new information systems. The "massive, centralised"
systems, designed, as at present, to handle the structured activities,
can't, because of the very nature of their activity, cope effectively with
what is unstructured. Still more significant, the advance of computers
from crunching numbers to exchanging information over machines
conforming to common standards, linked by networks and using
interchangeable and changeable software, represents a quantum leap
forward.
  There's no sensible argument with that Unisys statement: "Information is your key productive resource. Use it strategically and profit.
Ignore it and fail." However, that commandment doesn't answer the

crucial questions of how to use that key resource, and for what purpose. And in the answers now emerging lies the real excitement, the real payoff and the real revolution.

Chapter 22

THE CREATIVE INPUT

Behind brilliant advances in the processing of structured tasks lies brilliant unstructured work. The cases, reported in the previous chapter, of the insurance, elevator and supermarket companies which led their businesses into the information age are excellent examples. The information technologists performed prodigiously, no doubt, to get the insurance company's files organised by customer rather than policy number; to set up the centralised service system for the lift company; to supply working electronic point of sale systems to stores all over the world. But what set the technologists in motion?

It took a different order of intellectual achievement to spot that both the insurance company's commission system and the organisation of its files were winning short-term business at the expense of long-term, and to see that the two systems could be revised, with immediate benefit to the group's competitive stance. The authors comment that "Today many of that company's competitors are scrambling to install a similar setup ... but if they are just starting they face two or three years of costly systems programming to reorder their large, inflexible data files."

Winning such advances springs from winning ideas: from powerful insights. The lift company's management did equally well in spotting the defects in its system for managing service calls and in realising that reform offered the opportunity to kill two birds – golden eagles, at that – with a single stone: increasing market share (by improving both product and service) while reducing service costs.

Those retail companies that were first to move to EPOS gained like advantages. But even common systems universally applied can provide opportunities for executive insight. The latest large prizes in EPOS are going to manufacturers who realise that the information coming through the tills can provide more detailed information on true profitability of specific products than traditional measures can give. By using this information jointly, instead of sticking to the traditional

155

adversarial stance of the maker and the seller, both can gain increased profits.

Insight is the essence of unstructured achievement. It's the ability to assemble information (at which the workstation is uniquely fast and effective), to study the data (which the workstation assists by its ability to make cross-references), and to draw conclusions from the study that lead to change – to new understanding and new methods. Great thinkers and scientists achieve greatness through great insights: like Charles Darwin's observation in the very first sentence of *The Origin of Species*, that domesticated species, of both flora and fauna, differed from each other much more than species in the wild.

Thus, a dingo is much closer to a wolf than a dachshund to a Great Dane. There was nothing special about the observation – the *sight*. The special, human contribution was the notion that genetic mutation, deliberately pursued by human selection, must be analogous to the genetic mutation produced by what Darwin eventually called natural selection. That adds *insight* to sight, and the same process of extracting uncommon value from commonplace observation is the key to successful management in competitive conditions.

This is a whole dimension beyond what Bruns and McFarlan describe in the *Harvard Business Review* and the questions which, as they say, technology can now help to answer.

> Expensive data storage, sluggish retrieval, and complex systems that overwhelm the would-be users are all relics of the past. The technology now exists to transform the internal workings of the organisation ... Are plans and budgets made quickly and are they well communicated? Are decisions made in the right place? And if something changes, inside or outside the company, as it invariably will, can the control system adapt to the new requirements?

The two authors rightly place these questions, and their answers, in the context of decentralisation – of enabling senior managers to retain and exercise intelligent control of subsidiaries without relying on a bureaucratic apparatus that will stultify the independent powers of action that decentralisation is supposed to mobilise. As a writer in the *Guardian*, Andrew Cowie, has observed, "The pressure to break away from centralised systems is not only a product of technical development." The pressure is *social*, in a very deep and real sense of the word.

Cowie expressed that sense in an arresting question. "Is a company like an ant colony or an elephant? In other words, is it a social structure or is it organic, like a single living creature?" The metaphor may be a trifle mixed, since one biological view holds that an ant colony is not a society, but, indeed, a single living creature whose myriad apparently independent and individual existences are governed remorselessly by identical genes.

No doubt there are chief executives who dream of equal exemplary obedience from ostensibly decentralised corporations, staffed by utterly reliable managers who respond to the same programming and the same stimuli from the same central nervous system – the brain at the heart of the network. As Cowie pointed out, computer systems evolved much along the lines of this analogy: "The organic view proposed that although the left leg may not know what the right leg is doing, both are controlled by a brain which prevents each one from tripping the other up. Organic computer systems model the brain and nervous system in the form of centralised applications accessing integrated databases and a network of terminals."

What worked well for the corporate elephant (and would be fine for a colony of truly ant-like workers, managerial or otherwise), was also the only economic solution when mainframe computers, the sole alternative, were so expensive and complex. Since workers are becoming even more remote from ant-like behaviour, and computer alternatives have proliferated, the old solutions are neither necessary nor economic. Indeed, mainframe manufacturers have themselves been forced into extremely expensive software development to make their large machines perform more like, and much like, the smallest computers – the micros.

To quote *Fortune* magazine, "in a bid to protect its home turf", IBM in 1989 came up with a software bridge to allow "PCs, minis and mainframes to share programs and data", presenting an easy-to-use screen to all users. The screen closely resembles the technology developed at Xerox Corporation's Palo Alto Research Center and used by its own workstations and the Apple Macintosh. The expensive $8,000 per user IBM solution ("not for people who are price sensitive", says one industry expert) merely mimics what is already available on much cheaper networks.

To quote Cowie again, "the personal computer boom challenges the whole organic approach. Users can now store and process substantial volumes of data locally without connecting with the centralised mainframe at all." The need for accessibility has overtaken that for organic power at a time when, as *Fortune* writer Joel Dreyfuss puts it, "Unlike yesterday's computer specialists, today's managers use the machines as strategic tools."

Dreyfuss cites as examples a shipping executive getting an immediate read-out of the rates that all competitors are offering on a route and deriving an instantaneous guide to the price that will win the business. He can check on profitability, too, and learn at once which business to accept and which low-margin traffic to spurn. "Managers playing with such information have no patience with arcane commands, indecipherable screens and rigid barriers between databases. They want to reach all their information easily without having to worry about where it is stored or what brand of computer it's on."

The mainframe-oriented world resisted this user pressure for as long as it could. According to Cowie, "To many system developers local PC processing represents a corporate cancer which threatens the integrity of the organism. When they failed to kill it off, the PC was incorporated into the organic model by adding it to the mainframe network and restricting its use to data capture and analysis." This semi-Luddite attempt to hold back the tide has been defeated, not just by user pressure, but by technological revolution. As what Cowie calls "the gap in processing power" between PCs and mainframes has narrowed, so the cost gap in favour of PC-based solutions has widened.

Moreover, using PCs "as mainframe satellites exploits only a fraction of the potential. The widening gap between PC capacity and the use to which they are put casts doubt upon the organic system model" of the corporation. The organic system is fundamentally a control system – keeping the left leg of the elephant from tripping over the right. But in a social colony of intelligent, independent, individual, interacting ants, the controls become structured supports for unstructured work – which is carried out, what's more, in groups.

The way in which the strategy of information is driving management is shown by the exciting developments in a new category of software known as "groupware". In Silicon Valley, Robert Johansen, director of the New Technologies Program at the Institute for the Future, declares that "The business team is becoming the basic unit of measure rather than the individual." In June 1989, *Business Week* traced what were still, at that date, formative steps into Johansen's new age. "Interpersonal computing", "group dynamics", and so on are phrases that suggest the nature of a process that begins with work as simple as allowing all those in a network to annotate a document while leaving the original intact.

Moving up the ladder, another program "combines electronic mail, a group calendar and other functions to keep everyone on a network organised". Another software firm claims that its product will organise an entire small business or corporate department, routing work through an office – "from the receipt of an order, say, through the shipment of goods and billing ... the program would constantly track tasks waiting to be done and notify those responsible to get going."

All this would be done, note well, on a network of personal computers: the ant colony wins out over the elephant.

Yet another program "keeps a running log of an individual's work and appointments so that others can monitor what he or she is doing". That Big Brother-ish description sounds like the antithesis of true group working, an activity in which free men and women, freely associating, seek a better outcome than their single endeavours could achieve. Indeed, one sophisticated piece of groupware has been called "Naziware" by its critics. It comes from Action Technologies, whose C. Fernando Flores "believes that people would work together better if they labelled each of their interactions using a list of categories he developed".

The resulting program, The Co-ordinator, appears to impose far too structured a framework on activity that must be unstructured to achieve the creative strategic results at which groupware should be aiming. Programs are on the way that will help groups of people linked by computer to come closer and closer to the ideal of total, reinforced collaboration of people working together in the same room, poring over the same "papers". Already, in late 1989, two computers on the same network could show the same information – even while it was being changed; while Xerox Corporation was working on the addition of video to its groupware system, "so that people can see each other as they work together".

The development of software must be a crucial factor in unlocking the full strategic power of information, but the difficulties should not be underestimated. *Business Week* noted that one famous spreadsheet, Lotus 1–2–3, took five man-years to develop: its Release Three had taken eighty man-years – and was still incomplete at the time of the report – "partly because the new spreadsheet will have to work with many machines on a network".

Not surprisingly, feet have been dragged: resistance among software suppliers, however, like that of mainframe manufacturers, must crumble before the combined onslaught of true decentralisation, true group working and true understanding of the strategic contribution that can now be won from information systems. The *Guardian*'s Andrew Cowie talks of workers being "encouraged to change and improve their way of working. The company operates as an organisation of autonomous individuals."

It will be a messier organisation, but only in the sense that all unstructured work is messy. The very nature of being professional or knowledge workers means being interrupted as you work. Creative activities can never be wholly structured. People have to stop and think, have a discussion, exchange ideas and then come back to the issue – and this is precisely the to-and-fro activity for which the networked electronic office, based on the correct architecture, is ideally suited.

The Prussian general, Karl von Clausewitz, wrote that "War is the province of uncertainty: three-fourths of those things upon which action in war must be calculated, are hidden more or less in the clouds of great uncertainty." In unstructured work, dealing with ideas and tasks in the uncertain, warlike conditions of modern competition, unpredictability is of the essence. The office environment must suit both the people and the technology for the latter to benefit the former. In other words, if people have to fight either the technology or the organisation, nobody will win the real, external war for markets.

Yet the horizon is bright with promise. Raymond J. Noorda, chief executive of a network company, Novell, foresees highly versatile networks that, says *Business Week*, "will do automatically many of the things that humans now have to tell computers to do ... They'll talk, see, and almost feel." The challenge for top managements locked into traditional modes of management and thought is to exploit these new capabilities. That will be achieved by unlocking the powers of the networks to process strategic information and the ability of office workers at all levels to combine sight of data with insight to generate new competitive prowess.

Chapter 23

THE CHALLENGE OF COMPETITION

One of the major thrusts of the office revolution is that through raising productivity and reducing the numbers of people required, by installing true automation, overheads will be markedly reduced. It's a truism that successes in factory automation may result as much from better organisation of work as from the efficiency of high-tech hardware and software. Indeed, without the reorganisation, the high-tech powers simply can't be utilised.

As this book argues, the same is true of the office. While the revolution in equipment is itself driving companies towards far more effective and less costly modes of organising management (for which read office work), the better organisation was always available in essence. Many major corporations have gone through agonising exercises of white-collar staff cuts in order to survive financial crisis – and there's very little evidence that any important sacrifices have been made in corporate capability.

Many of the cuts have been made in head offices, whose relative decline became inevitable with the all but universal trend towards devolving power to discrete units with greater autonomy and responsibility. That reflects a cause which embodies the greatest challenge of them all: the challenge of competition. There has been a crucial shift across virtually all markets, for goods and services alike, from the supply of needs (musts) to the satisfaction of desires (wants), or from producer dominance to saturation. The resulting battle for markets has placed a higher premium than ever on obtaining the lowest possible costs for the largest possible market share.

The business with lower overheads is a more effective competitor. Reduction in overheads had been a necessary target of high-class managers ever since the concepts of direct and indirect costs were first properly understood. For a long time, finance departments have been earning their keep, and covering their costs, by using information systems to generate the maximum amount of cash (i.e. to minimise the amount of working capital) which is required to operate the company; their systems are also supposed to optimise the return on the cash balances. But such gains, while vital, do nothing to affect the fundamental competitiveness of the firm, which hinges on how well it serves its markets and at what cost/price relationship.

In the coming phase of the office revolution, the power of information technology will be harnessed directly to the achievement of competitive advantage – not only by devising better strategies (which will also follow), but by eliminating time wasted in all parts of the supply chain. In fact, the future tense in the last sentence is misleading. Competitive advantage is already being won, and has been won for some time past, by companies which are aggressively using the office as an area for speeding up output.

Information processed in the office has always been the foundation of improvements in manufacturing. You cannot take advantage of the enormous gains available from reducing a product line unless you know which segments of the market, offering the highest returns, are the ones on which to concentrate. If you do know, you can exploit the fact that cutting variety by 30% raises productivity by 30% and lowers costs by 17%; a further halving in variety, moreover, achieves a 75% rise in productivity, a 30% cost reduction, and a fall in the breakeven point to under half of capacity.

Nor can you advance from this strategy (as the Japanese did in seeking to widen their markets) to the optimum combination of scale-related and variety-driven costs unless you can run rapidly through the complex trade-offs. But in describing the importance of these stages of Japan's brilliant strategic development, George Stalk Jr, in a prize-winning article published in the *Harvard Business Review* in the summer of 1988, was only setting the stage for an even more important breakthrough: the aggressive use of time as a competitive weapon.

He cites the case of Toyota Motor Manufacturing and Toyota Motor Sales, which until 1982 were quite separate companies, both with wonderful records of achievement. The sales company had achieved the critical breakthrough in the United States market, overtaking Volkswagen after a long and epic struggle. But where Toyota's factories contained some of the world's most efficient offices – part of the key to its ability to make a car in two days – the sales company, which consisted exclusively of office workers, was so much less efficient that it added thirteen to twenty-four days to the time required to fill a customer's order.

Stalk reports that 20 to 30% of a car's final cost was incurred in sales and distribution – "more than it cost Toyota to manufacture the car!" After the two separate Toyota companies were merged in 1982, it took only eighteen months to remove all the Sales company directors, some of whom were never replaced. A common way in which offices build up useless time elapsed is through processing orders in batches, which means waiting until the batch is large enough. The motor men now in charge knew that reducing the size of batches was the only way to speed up the information flow.

"The solution," writes Stalk, "came from a company-developed computer system that tied its salespeople directly to the factory scheduling operation. This link bypassed several levels of the sale and distribution function and enabled the modified system to operate with very small batches." The expected benefit was to halve the sales and distribution cycle to two to three weeks nationally (two *days* in the crowded Tokyo and Osaka regions). "But by 1987 Toyota had reduced system responsiveness to eight days, including the time required to make the car."

Similar benefits are available to every company which has an order cycle. Detailed knowledge of the role the office plays in manufacturing costs (through the delays imposed by inefficient office work) dates back to 1958. In that year, Jay W. Forrester of MIT, also writing in the *Harvard Business Review*, recorded the life-cycle of "the planning loop" as an order moved from the retailer to the distributor to the factory and back again – and the results were dramatic in their implications.

The total cycle took nineteen weeks. The first three weeks of the order's life were spent building up in the office at the retail outlet. A further half-week of time was lost in the post, so to speak. The distributor's office added another two weeks to the order's life; and the mail needed another half-week. Eight weeks were required by the factory and its warehouse before the final three weeks could be spent in transit. In all, more than six weeks – a third of the whole cycle – was spent in paperwork and its transmission.

The office revolution should have changed this pattern radically. Orders can now be transmitted electronically direct to the factory, bypassing the distributor altogether; even if the latter remains in the cycle, there's no reason why his system should add any significant delays. Order batching is no more necessary than the postal service. Yet only a few companies were yet taking advantage of the potential when Stalk wrote – to judge by another case which he reported.

He found an industrial door manufacturer, Atlas, which, after all of ten years of life, marked by three times the growth rate of the industry as a whole, had become its leader. Yet its competitors had still not grasped the point expressed in one of man's older adages: that time is money. Lead-times in the industry, which has very few standard products, average four months: those at Atlas run for only a few weeks because it has "structured its order-entry, engineering, manufacturing and logistics systems to move information and products quickly and reliably". Much of the gain, as Forrester's work of thirty years ago demonstrated, could be made at the start of the operation.

Stalk writes: "Traditionally, when customers, distributors or salespeople called a door manufacturer with a request for price and delivery they would have to wait more than one week for a response." The wait was longer still if the door was neither in stock, in the schedule or in engineering. But after investing in an automated system for order entry, engineering, pricing and scheduling, "Atlas can price and schedule 95% of its incoming orders while the callers are still on the telephone."

The crucial truth to emerge from Stalk's excellent article is contained in its title: "Time – the Next Source of Competitive Advantage". To gain an advantage, however, not only do you require a winning edge: you also need an opponent who won't match your gains. The office revolutionaries like Atlas can, however, count on slow and conservative reaction from competitors who haven't grasped the enormous contribution that office systems can make to lower costs – or that old-fashioned ways can make to excess spending.

A vital consideration, as Forrester pointed out, is that the longer the cycle time, the greater the uncertainty. If you take only two days to supply a customer, like Toyota in Tokyo and Osaka, you only need to forecast demand two days ahead. The precision is far greater than it can ever be with a nineteen-week cycle, where the factory is responding to demand as it was nearly five months ago. Any efforts to build output to cut delivery delays, or reduce production to cut stock, can wildly destabilise the work flow through the factory.

In any event, the factory in the Forrester model, remember, ate up only eight of the nineteen weeks – meaning that elimination of the six weeks of wasted time in the offices outside the plant could produce savings equivalent to three-quarters of the total time spent in manufacture. Much of that surplus time, moreover, will be wasted not just by the quantum of office work, but by its inferior quality. Better systems in factory offices, reducing the quantum and raising the quality at one blow, can often eliminate more unnecessary time than automation on the production line itself.

The office can be seen, not only as an information machine, but a time machine. Time is its real fuel: the time taken over the basic processes of receiving, analysing and processing information, plus that spent in thought, decision and creation. Left to human beings, the structured office processes are laborious and time-consuming, which is why the mundane work of payroll, sales ledgers, reservation systems and so on had to be automated. The new dimension, though, moves beyond mere saving of time to the concentration of effort into small parcels of time: making possible what could never have been envisaged before.

Take the initials MSP, which stand for "marketing and sales productivity", a phrase coined by Rowland T. Moriarty and Gordon S. Swartz in the *Harvard Business Review* of January–February 1989. "Marketing" subsumes a host of activities: the authors list national account management, direct sales, telemarketing, direct mail, literature fulfilment, advertising, customer service, dealer and distributor relationships. In quite small companies, they cite better than 100% returns on the investment in office systems.

The article argues that "MSP systems support productivity in two ways. First, automation of selling and direct marketing support tasks boosts the efficiency of the sale and marketing staff. Second, automating the collection and analysis of marketing information improves the timeliness and the quality of marketing and sales executives' decision-making." Repetitive tasks are transferred to the computer, while better information strengthens the ability of sales and marketing people to make effective use of their enlarged time.

The productivity results in an office can be as profitable as any saving in a factory. In the mid-eighties Xerox Corporation developed its own MSP system for use in the south of the United States. According to Swartz and Moriarty (who once worked for Xerox), the company "credits the system with a 10 to 20% gain in sales force productivity and with trimming $3 million off the 1987 marketing support and overhead budget. By automating sales and administration support tasks, Xerox has given its salespeople more time to sell."

That encapsulates the objectives of the office revolution. It removes from people the tasks for which machines are better equipped. It gives to people the time which is the ultimate governor of their effectiveness, and enables them to convert time into results far more readily. The reduction in the order cycle at Toyota is paralleled by the cut in the "turnaround time for leads" at Hewlett-Packard, thanks to a system called QUILTS – Qualified Lead Tracking System. This has cut the timespan "from as much as fourteen weeks to as little as forty-eight hours".

Exactly the same order of benefit has been won at the Remington Arms division of Du Pont. The national rollout of pricing and promotional programmes, which used to take a couple of weeks, now takes under two days. A clothing company mentioned by Moriarty and Swartz gave lap-tops to the people: they could use their PCs to get inventory and order status information, held in the corporate database. Not only was the order cycle reduced from two weeks to three days, but the improved service boosted sales by 10%.

As in a factory, every benefit reinforces every other benefit. The more the office-based executives know about the market and the customers, because more information has been collected in the database, the better able they are to direct their marketing spend towards the more profitable objectives. For instance, direct marketing is cheap, but not especially productive – a 2% response is considered excellent. The better the quality of the database (that is, the greater its relevance to the offer), the higher the response rate, and the greater the payoff.

Resistance to change in such circumstances seems especially ridiculous. But marketing and salespeople, like all workers, are frightened by change. The fright has to be overcome in view of the obvious benefits of highlighting and co-ordinating information, such as all customer contacts, however made; the current status of all sales activities; where all leads come from; what leads are being followed up internally or by distributors; all purchasers; what they bought, and when. Merely to list such information is to recognise its power and its necessity in an intensely competitive environment – one dominated by demanding customers who buy in fragmented markets where competitors seek to attract discretionary spending with highly differentiated offerings.

But there's a price to pay, and according to Moriarty and Swartz, it's a steep one: perhaps $3 million to $5 million for a firm with 500 people selling and with telemarketing, fulfilment and direct mail operations. In a company which has already entered the office revolution, however, there might be no additional hardware costs, which on the authors' figures would eliminate between $2.5 million and $3.5 million of spending on the salesforce alone. Since marketing and sales account for 15 to 35% of *total* corporate costs, and service activities represent 75% to 85% of the total value added, the expenditure must pay for itself if the authors are only half right in assessing the benefits.

The gains will be measured in time. Telemarketers at a Californian uniform supply firm used to take a day for thirty-five to forty calls, which yielded about one sale a *month*: now fifty to sixty calls a day yield three to four sales. Hewlett-Packard can get sales leads into the field in twenty-four hours, as against one to two weeks. A printer's customers can price and place orders with a single call. And just as the adoption of time-based strategies has taken the Japanese thrust into world markets a surge forward, by using the same principle, early

166

adopters of MSP "have gained superior competitive advantage". The marketing and sales offices have turned from overhead to engines of growth and profit – and that is the real name of the revolution.

Chapter 24

THE PROGRAMME FOR SUCCESS

Even in the late summer of 1989, a highly informed executive of a firm making minicomputers could still refer to workstations as exclusive to engineers – at a time when the executive workstation had not only become reality, but was plainly about to revolutionise managerial work (including, no doubt, the executive's own labours).

This single example raises a small corner of the carpet to expose the dusty mass of conservative resistance to the fact that "Information systems will lead to improved measurement, more cohesive incentives, and substantially better communications and co-ordination", and that "as a consequence, organisations will be flatter, more differentiated, more accountable, and more responsive". Those words, from McKinsey & Company's Carter F. Bales, are a somewhat muted description of what sounds like (and will be) a sea-change in corporate management. But their muted tone is echoed by a definitely sombre warning about "very costly" systems that "deliver no advantage", and "cause major unanticipated implementation problems".

Worse still, top managers are often "damned if they do, damned if they don't". Bales says that consequently these would-be leaders are often "frustrated by the inability of their companies to move forward". His cautions appear in the foreword to a McKinsey Paper, by John L. Cecil and Eugene A. Hall, entitled "When IT really matters to business strategy". The main argument of this book is that IT from this moment on matters to business strategy all the time: that strategy cannot be formed effectively without drawing on the powers of systems to discover, analyse and communicate information. Have these two highly experienced consultants discovered a weakness in the case?

"In general," they wrote in the autumn of 1988, "so-called 'strategic' information technical expenditures have *not* created competitive advantage." They acknowledge that certain "big wins" do exist, but rightly observe that, to prove the point, the same "strategic systems" are "usually trotted out – correctly or incorrectly". It's characteristic of management writing to seize three or four heroic examples to prove a case while ignoring the 96 or 97 that might lead to different conclusions.

But both the "big wins" (like the SABRE reservation system devised by American Airlines) and the failures (like rival insurance company and bank schemes to cut costs by computerisation, which cancelled each other out) are beside the real point. The use of what the authors call "stand-alone" applications can indeed "improve performance by increasing the effectiveness of specific operational functions". But these gains will over time be imitated by any competitors who want to stay in business; and then "the net impact of IT-driven homogenisation" will very probably be "a reduction in total industry cost and profitability".

In other words, the cost savings will be passed on to the customer, and returns on the expensive investment in new technology will disappoint. But such stand-alone investments are exclusively in structured activities, where the argument from competitive advantage isn't necessary. If technology makes it possible to process structured work faster, more accurately and at lower cost, the strategic issue arises only in the bluntest possible form. Stick with the old system, and you're stuck, not with competitive advantage but competitive disadvantage – and with that you cannot live, but only die.

Today's and tomorrow's Office Systems Technology is the antithesis of the stand-alone philosophy, just as "network" is its antonym. The McKinsey authors cite some more hopeful examples where companies have used IT to "leverage existing business strengths" through "scale economies, product differentiation and unique institutional skills". For instance, "a major packaged goods company faced the problem of distributing enough of its perishable food product to meet highly volatile consumption patterns". Its answer was "an IT-based system to improve sales forecasting by using historical information to analyse complex demand swings under different types of marketing plans. The system showed that demand was actually quite predictable."

Branch operation costs fell by 20%, and capacity utilisation improved, without the risk of being out of stock. This is a classic case of good information driving out bad. The company had created its own mini-crisis by believing the false information that demand was unpredictable. The purpose of a company-wide information system is to provide simultaneously the means of challenge and the ammunition to support it. The information itself, however, is neutral – effective action on the information, mobilised by the strategic use of the system, makes the crucial difference.

This vital point was demonstrated over the long years of the greatest military confrontation the world has ever seen: the 1939–45 war. From an early date, the cracking of the Enigma code enabled the allies to intercept and understand all German messages. Yet despite overwhelming superiority in war production, raw materials and manpower, fighting against an enemy whose efforts were fatefully divided between two fronts (three, if you include the obscene subjection of the occupied nations and races), the defeat of the Third Reich was long, laborious, bloody and strategically flawed.

The thought of what might have happened without the Enigma information is horrifying. Accounts of the strategic fiascos (such as Arnhem) identify the same cause: choice of strategy *before* full information has been gathered and considered, refusal to reconsider strategy *after* its decision even when fuller information undermines its foundations. Such refusal in turn reflects hierarchical organisation – even field commanders who doubted the Arnhem strategy were unable to influence the decisions of Field Marshal Montgomery and his staff.

That is the opposite of what happens in the "flatter, more differentiated, more accountable, and more responsive" organisations which Carter Bales rightly foresaw being created by IT. To quote the McKinsey Paper, "The most powerful uses of IT to enhance existing non-technology based strengths arise, not from straightforward automation of activities, but from integrating various aspects of a business ... across products or customers to create a customer focus, across business functions to co-ordinate business system elements, or across geographies to leverage a company's global presence."

As the paper points out, internal company frontiers typically act as barriers, often with the former finality of the Berlin Wall. Other companies will readily emulate an automated system for any routine activity: they will find it far harder, thanks to their own cultural hangups, to break down the barriers with the genuine integration offered by IT. "As a result, integrative applications tend to have great power and lead to genuinely sustainable advantage" even when exploiting existing business. In developing new opportunities the power of Office Systems Technology is still greater.

It has to be said that the examples given by Cecil and Hall are more stand-alone than integrative – American Airlines' SABRE system (again) or the use by banks of information captured in the mortgage application process to cross-sell other financial products. The cross-selling opportunities offer potential profits per customer that come near to those on the original mortgage. But this benefit offers nothing like the gains which one investment bank has won through a "computer-based analytic/decision support system" that has produced "ongoing wholesale changes to the way it conducts business".

The Programme for Success

This company, in "building and refining the system" kept on learning more about the business and its customers – including the realisation that, unless the latter understood the value of the system, it wouldn't have any customers. Every forward step taken, from customer education seminars to training videos and "innovative new securities", was a potential source of additional market share (which the company concerned had in fact obtained as a due reward for its strategic IT efforts).

The McKinsey Paper doesn't give enough detail to allow comment on this particular case. But the conclusions the authors draw are fascinating – including the importance of being a leader, and not a follower, when technology and the business environment are changing. As they write, "Change creates opportunities for competitors who 'move early'." They draw three principles from this observation.

1. Continually re-examine all elements of the business system in light of new technology and new applications of existing technology.
2. Commit substantial technical and non-technical resources to the development of IT-based applications early in the game, when real competitive gains appear feasible.
3. Recognise that neither the "ultimate" approach nor the organisational support it requires can be fully identified beforehand.

These principles, bear in mind, come from authors who began their paper by expressing considerable reservations about the prospects of winning competitive advantage through strategic investment in IT. For them to end by advocating a measure of sometimes flying blind, of adopting new technology because it's there, and of perpetual change is an extraordinary conversion. They appreciate its extent themselves: "These principles contrast greatly with the approach best suited to stand-alone applications, where rigorous economic analysis is needed to select technologies and determine the optimal point of adoption."

Instead, if the endeavour is to create "new experience-based advantage", they ask managers "to commit resources early – long before they know the size of the total IT investment, the full end-product or the scope of the impact". It's doubtful whether the most ebullient computer salesman ever paid a commission has demanded so open-handed and open-ended a commitment. The tenor of the paper has turned full circle: but, then, so has the concept of business organisation.

To survive and thrive, strategies for keeping competitive in an industry with declining profitability, for leveraging existing strengths, and for creating entirely new ways to conduct business (all listed by the authors) have become mandatory requirements – not for companies which are in crisis, or anything like it, but for all firms whose future prosperity rests on the ability to achieve strategic change. The change may well have to be as radical as that of any turnround. The issue isn't to find the right strategy for IT, but to develop an organisational strategy, which can be supported by IT, that will empower the business to generate strong strategic initiatives across the board.

Cecil and Hall's concluding advice really parts company with the specific object of IT and moves into something at once the same and different: the management of change. Businesses advancing (instead of being dragged) into the next century will need "top management with a broad vision of how its company can be reshaped ... and a willingness to rebuild major parts of the current business system". They will also need "highly skilled business and technology managers with a deep and shared understanding", together with an "orientation towards active experimentation".

I have left out the specific references to IT in the above quotes because the authors are so incontrovertibly right in saying that "ultimately, the strategic use of information technology is a business decision", and not a technological one. It is a decision to master change in the updated spirit of Heraclitus, who declared, five centuries before Christ, that "The only permanent thing in life is change." In one sense, the decision is easy to make, since the alternative – to rest, and rest content – with the *status quo*, is not tenable.

In another sense, the decision is hard, because change always involves the unknown, and man, a superstitious animal, seeks certainties. This book, however, has sought to establish that the office revolution is no longer a matter of gambling with risky expenditures, but of exploiting what certainly works. Equally certainly, it is the only way in which the business of offices and managers will be conducted in a new and near future which is, to all intents and purposes, the present.

It's a truism – already noted – that technological revolutions only take place, not when the technology is ripe, but when conditions favour or demand its adoption. The initial investment in business computers came in time to save large companies from being swamped by clerical demands. The second wave performed the same rescue for medium-sized and smaller companies. Now the third wave has arrived just in time to cope with complexity – to achieve sensible choices among a constantly increasing range of business options to which an equally wide and widening number of inter-related disciplines have to be applied.

The Programme for Success

The demanding conditions of complex markets impose seven key requirements on the firm and its managers. They have to compete, which goes without saying; to establish real market leadership, going beyond market share into all the intangibles which influence customer perception; to form and meet challenging targets; to achieve the highest standards of professionalism; to defend core businesses with unshakable tenacity; to innovate constantly in product and process; and to accept and adapt to change.

All these elements depend on finding the answers to detailed, probing questions – and acting on the answers, continuously guided by feedback, which is also information. In the office of the past/present, even when the elements are understood, and the questions phrased, finding the answers is laborious, slow and sometimes impossible: that is equally true of the feedback. In the office of the future/present, the networked system becomes the management system, and both answers and feedback can become slick, swift and certain. There are problems, true: but they are not those of static impotence in face of changing market powers.

Chapter 25

THE MANAGEMENT OF INFORMATION

What new problems are raised by the decision to network the office or offices? A number are highlighted in Sara Kiesler's important article in the *Harvard Business Review* (January–February 1986). Here are some of them:

1. How do you ensure that the office doesn't just generate more and more exchange of less and less useful information?
2. Who decides what information gets collected and distributed to whom?
3. What criteria should govern the selection of distributed information?
4. How do you maintain the correct balance between internal and external information?
5. Who has access to what corporate data?
6. Who controls the use of the network – and why?
7. What steps can be taken to ensure that electronic messages are not only sent, not only received, but acted on?
8. If the answers to the above questions involve several people, how are their decisions and actions to be co-ordinated?
9. Should the network be used as a social device – carrying messages devoid of business content that nevertheless bring people together in an "electronic community"?
10. How far can the network be used, instead of face-to-face discussion, in making important decisions?

None of the questions is easy to answer, and it's tempting to fall back on the same kind of reply that is logically justified in the cost-benefit assessment of networks. Once you have computers on the desktops, as you must have, for information access alone, then networking and other facilities are manifestly both logical and economic. Once you have networks, the ten tough questions will, somehow or other, answer themselves.

Kiesler sums up this loose, if comforting conclusion in these words: "In the computerised organisation, more people will have information that always existed and some people will have new information. Computer networks will change existing groups and will create new, electronic groups. People will relate to one another in different ways, and the dynamics of decision-making may change." Her plea for a "light-handed policing policy" suggests letting nature take its course as far as possible – simply because undue constraints will limit the potential of a system which, in any case, will make up some, maybe many, of its rules as it goes along.

But the fundamental issue behind all ten questions is quite obvious. It is a matter of delegation, or to use another word, sharing. The delegator (although the matter is seldom viewed in this way) is a sharer. He gives some of his authority, his work, to somebody else, without altogether relinquishing his property rights. He can, for example, grab back the delegated work. He may be held responsible for its quality and achievement, anyway. Traditionally, proliferation of information has been curbed (but also often created) by top-down methods. Paperwork bonfires are always initiated from above, often in face of extreme opposition lower down.

That's because the files and the reports symbolise the delegated powers. Remove them, and even if the symbols have become wholly symbolic, i.e. useless, the possessor feels weakened, emasculated. The idea of management work cascading down from the top is intrinsic to the whole concept of hierarchy. It penetrates to the fundamentals of corporate management. But before investigating the profound depths this implies, the management of computer systems themselves raises more immediate issues. They are not problems with which senior management has been much concerned in the past. Like the organisation and control of the despatch system, those of the information system have been delegated.

The role and importance of the chief delegatee, the "manager of information systems", or the bearer of some similar title, have inevitably risen in stature as information has moved to stage centre. But now the drama is unfolding in a different way. "Decentralised computing is sweeping business like a wave rolling onto a beach", wrote John J. Donovan in the *Harvard Business Review* (Sept–Oct 1988). Economic considerations, he pointed out, were among the factors making the advance as unstoppable as that tidal wave. Comparing a mainframe with a personal computer, the average cost per mip (millions of instructions per second) comes down by 98% – from nearly $200,000 to $4,000.

This dramatic decline in hardware costs, accompanied by lower

175

software development expenses, is quite enough to explain the movement away from central and centrally managed systems. The organisational potential of the new technology only intensifies the pressures for change; Donovan, an associate professor at MIT's Sloan School of Management, identifies centripetal forces within organisations themselves. "Employees want to operate their own systems, in their own way, and when it's most convenient for them," and he regards this development (rightly enough) as fundamentally healthy.

"The migration of computing power from corporate headquarters to divisions, plants and desktops," he writes, "promises to reduce costs, enhance competitiveness, and renew organisational creativity." As this book has argued, these three aims are the objective and justification of the office revolution. The answers to the ten questions posed in this chapter will have to come from the bottom up, almost by definition. But, as Donovan points out, this process must be disciplined. You don't want to "wind up with hundreds of isolated applications – what I call information islands – unable to share data".

Equally, you don't want, while suppressing too much non-conformity, to suppress the very vitality and local system ownership that are the essence of the revolution. Donovan argues that the resolution of the tangle lies in the evolution of the information systems manager, known in the US as the chief information officer. The "new breed" of senior information manager will have a new definition, if not a new title: "network manager".

The argument is irrefutable. Whatever the title, unless these people convert themselves from overlords of vast hardware and software investments and budgets, and concentrate instead on networks, their companies cannot enter the age of decentralised computing. The culture shock for IT professionals mimics that for the whole bureaucratic, hierarchical organisation framework. Like other senior managers, the top IT executive has to make surrender after surrender. Authority over hardware and software purchases is the first thing to go, but its loss is only part of a much wider surrender: of order for chaos. When anybody and everybody can buy programs and machines within their own budgets, anarchy has replaced the absolute control that corporate information people once wielded.

Donovan describes this as the "Big Brother" mode: "large mainframes available only to data-processing professionals run programs designed and written by centralised software teams." As he says, "Today this set of policies is an organisational and technological dinosaur": the exact description of the corporations it was designed to serve. This particular type of dinosaur has evolved, unlike the dinosaur of history. But the next stage, the "helping hand" mode, with

176

the hardware distributed, the users setting priorities, and the central experts doing all the technical work is simply not responsive enough.

Donovan has a horror story about a state government whose frustrated users beat backlogs by various unauthorised initiatives: "Ultimately the government wound up with dozens of databases and spreadsheets that could not feed into its central computer. It still has not unravelled the mess." Try to maintain control as the organisation moves towards controlled chaos, in other words, and you get uncontrolled chaos. Probably the most natural course for companies that haven't fully understood the new imperatives is the "watchdog" phase, in which you let people get on with their own computing, but keep ultimate control in the centre by establishing an overriding authority, with standard operating systems and programming language, and the operation of "frequent and rigorous audits".

Donovan says this generates "the most severe built-in tensions" of any model he's studied "and is therefore the least stable" – and you can certainly see why. Only an organisation belonging to the clan of "large inflexible bureaucracies with clear lines of authority and hierarchy" could even attempt to live within this system. It has no place in a world which is moving, because move it must, from bureaucracy to entrepreneurial college, from inflexibility to suppleness, from clear lines of authority to a criss-cross grid of relationships, from hierarchy to the authority of expertise.

Donovan's solution has the supreme virtue of being right. Like all right answers, in the natural sciences, the arts, or engineering, it also looks right: it has, in his phrase, "structural elegance". The problem of exercising control of everyday computing is neatly resolved by abandoning the attempt. Control rests with use: the user has responsibility for what he uses. What's left to the network manager, however, is perhaps the trickiest set of problems ever presented to IT professionals.

For the office revolution to be fully effective there must be perfect connection at three levels. Individual workstations, PCs, minicomputers and mainframes, plus other devices such as shared database processes, must have perfect individual, physical connection to a network. Through the network there must be perfect connection between all systems. And (most difficult of all) there must be perfect connection between all applications running on any of these systems. In a perfect situation, where every piece of hardware and software fitted perfectly together, with the same operating systems, data storage and exchange, and mainframe-to-mini-to-workstation connections, the task would be easy. In a welter of different standards, though, the company has its work cut out to turn the Tower of Babel into an intelligible, universal language.

The trend towards true compatibility, however, is inevitable, both through the development of single-vendor networks (in which one office supplier installs the whole set-up) and through the belated evolution of open, multi-vendor standards. How it's done is less important than getting it done. Donovan is emphatic that "a network manager's most basic responsibility is to build and maintain a robust data communications infrastructure – the physical network. That minimises interruptions and downtime." The technicalities of this work – the modems, multiplexers, local area network connectors and so on – will fade into obscurity, of course: the supply of physical links, like that of water or gas, will be taken for granted by the user.

That will also be true of the next, more difficult aspect of linkage: making sure that all systems anywhere in the outfit are integrated "under a consistent, easy-to-use interface". Without that, some of the ten questions raised at the start cannot be answered. The corporate staff can't monitor the efficiency of the network's components, or safeguard the secrets it contains, or ensure that every part of the network that could use a new application actually can do so.

This isn't the same thing as "applications connectivity". Anything that's part of the system must be able to work with anything else in the system. But getting "the hundreds of applications running on the network" to "freely exchange information" is another and far more challenging matter. As Donovan points out, even if the computers and software in the network are nearly identical, the constant changes in applications will endanger the ability of one application to feed into another.

The example he gives can serve as both warning of the difficulties and demonstration of the potential benefits. You're a "relationship banker", meaning that you seek to establish a connection with an individual client to cover all his or her associations with the bank. Obviously, the commercial prizes in establishing such a relationship are great. But you can't analyse, evaluate and change the client's whole investment portfolio – generating large commissions for the bank in the process – unless you can mobilise information from the several complex systems that control respectively the customer's mortgage, fixed interest investments, current accounts and loans.

Without strict procedures, the relationship banker might run into a brick wall. In that context, it's "quite encouraging", as Donovan says, to learn that major organisations, like the American Red Cross, have made progress with "application filters that translate between different systems on the network, hide each computer's particular characteristics and adjust for application changes". It's still more encouraging to learn that eventually the physician will be able to heal itself: that expert systems, carried within the network, "may be able to detect and adjust automatically for application changes affecting the rest of the network".

The difficulties make the case for single-vendor networks seem stronger. But that's not the main point. The thrust of the office of the future is that communication will take over as the central function of the electronic network, and that "sheer processing performance", the god in the temple for the whole of the computer age until now, will be displaced, toppled from its pedestal. Managing the inter-communications will take over as the means of control and direction, while the use of the hardware and software united by the network will rest with the user.

The relationship banker will be no more aware of the electronic conduits that assemble his client's financial data than he is of the air traffic network that guides his plane safely to its destination. He will only care about getting there. And he will.

The responsibility for getting the information, however, will be his – not that of Donovan's "network manager". Understanding the complex issues of a day in which there aren't too many simple ones requires superb information. That in turn demands being proactive, not reactive: managing information, not being managed by it. The essential equipment of modern managers includes knowing what information they need, how they want it, where they want it, and when.

The essential task of the information manager is to meet these internal "customers" more than halfway, in the interests of an over-riding purpose. That's expressed in an observation by Peter Drucker – that knowing what to do in management is easy: it's doing it that's hard. The task of information management in an age of complex competition is to provide knowledge easily, and to make the hard task of turning it into action easier as well. There's no doubt about the ability of the new technology: the doubt and difficulty hang over its management, and even more over the management of those who give the system life.

BOOK VI
The Management of Change

Chapter 26

THE UNSTRUCTURED UPHEAVAL

All 35 mm colour print films now on sale adhere (unlike computer hardware and software) to a common standard. Even though Eastman Kodak, Fuji, Konica and private label suppliers are locked in ferocious rivalry, their films are all chemically compatible and can all be processed on identical machines. The operator has only to set the machine according to pre-determined instructions, feed in the films, and wait for the identical machines to achieve identical results.

Only, as every amateur photographer knows, they don't. Significant variances, enough to make a mediocre snap good, and vice versa, occur between machines – or rather between operators. In theory, the latter should make no difference. In practice, the discrepancies can be as great as in the days before standardisation and automation. The relevance of this familiar experience to office automation is profound. Moving over to machines can be used to eliminate human influence altogether – or as near as possible to altogether. But that will not get the best out of the system. Nor will it get the best out of the humans who remain in employment.

That lesson may take a long time in the learning, to judge by the story of one large corporation, itself a major manufacturer of computers, that established a brand-new office for its value-added networks group in a new business park. It employed 150 staff, described as highly skilled. These experts were provided with all the technical infrastructure they could possibly require: every workstation had two power outlets, two telecom points, two data terminal points and a network connection point.

The layout was open – an inevitable choice in such circumstances. But the company culture was closed, According to a writer who had visited the site, the company "frowns" on staff "stopping for a chat". It "encourages use of screen-to-screen electronic mail for passing information, and expects face-to-face discussion to be set up by a prior telephone call". There are rooms of various sizes to accommodate these pre-arranged meetings: but the company also "does not recognise territorial rights", so "any available work station can be used for a one-to-one meeting".

The corporate "culture" in this case immediately calls to mind Shoshana Zuboff's story, in her book, *In the Age of the Smart Machine*, about the two office workers who contrived a hole in the partitions which separated them - simply so that they could see evidence of another human being. The possibility exists in all automation of eliminating the human factor completely. A perhaps apocryphal account tells of a party of academics visiting Japan who were disconcerted to find that no interviews had been arranged with the employees at the showpiece automated plant they had come to see. They wanted, like Zuboff, to interrogate people to find out their reactions to the smart factory at first hand.

They put their demand to the company president, who replied flatly, "No people!" This rude rejection, to the visitors' surprise and discomfort, was repeated several times, until they got the point: the plant employed no people. The object of most automation is to do more, and more efficient, work, with fewer people: and the fewest amount of people is none. But even automatic factories will require engineers; and behind these last blue-collar survivors will be the white-collar ranks in the offices. The issue so far as they are concerned is clear. Will they be treated as the servants or the masters of the system?

The most painful of Zuboff's brilliant pages are those with drawings that show the before and after views of office workers as seen by themselves: a happy, smiling transfer assistant (the transfers being those of stocks and bonds) before the system was installed; after, a back view dominated by a crudely drawn, dominating screen with a damning legend – "The after picture is only the back of my head, because it is a non-person."

Then there's a benefits analyst for a dental insurance firm. The first sketch shows a sunny landscape seen through a window, somebody behind labelled "fellow worker", and the analyst talking on the phone – "Hi, this is Ann. Can I help you?" The "after" shows a desk, a terminal, and nothing else. "She is all by herself . . . You are just out there." Another subject in the same job draws an Elysian view of shining sun (again), smiles and flowers: the only sign of work is a phone. "After" shows office equipment ("ring, ring, ring" and "keep up MPH"), with a scowling face looking over the partition.

This is almost laughably reminiscent of the computer company culture referred to above: "My supervisor is frowning because we shouldn't be talking. I have on the stripes of a convict. It's all true. It feels like a prison in here." It has to be said that the work these women did before the system took over was by no means inspiring. Walking over to ledgers and making manual entries day after day is hardly an exercise satisfying to the deeper human aspirations. What they missed in the new environment, however, was very human: the human contact which has always distressed the tidy-minded.

Zuboff quotes the "scientific management" pioneer William Henry Leffingwell, who wanted to create an office in which work would move in straight lines "without the necessity of the clerk even rising from his seat ... It should not be overlooked that while a clerk is not at his desk he may be working, but he is not doing clerical work effectively." To remove any need for clerks to move, Leffingwell needed a whole battery of devices. Zuboff lists "layout, standardisation of methods, a well-organised messenger service, desk correspondence distributors, reliance on written instructions, delivery bags, pneumatic tubes, elevators, automatic conveyors, belt conveyors, cables, telautographs, telephones, phonographs, buzzes, bells and horns".

All these are subsumed by the computerised network. The office worker can be isolated more effectively than Leffingwell can ever have imagined. With no more need for initiative or human contact than Charlie Chaplin's factory worker in *Modern Times*, she sits at her screen and at regular short intervals presses the ENTER button on the keyboard. The Zuboff terminology for such work is "acting-on". The worker gets given a piece of information and processes it. This is "structured" work at its purest and most limiting.

Zuboff points out, however, that when a lower-order office job is "enriched, it tends to resume its treadmill position in direct line of descent from the executive function" – the workers start "acting-with" (that is, relating to other people in order to carry out their own jobs). There's plenty of evidence that, the higher the degree of "acting with", the more effectively the "acting on" takes place.

Because of the difficulties of truly measuring effective output in the office, factory cases are the best to hand. Zuboff cites the expense tracking system at Tiger Creek Mill (her pseudonym for one of the paper mills she investigated). Instead of the traditional approach, taking initiative up and away from the operators, the managers involved pushed "accurate, detailed, real-time information on operating expenses" down into the hands of the operators – they "could make the decisions that were once the exclusive domain of managers and engineers".

According to one of the latter, in setting up the system, the operators "controlled things no one else even conceived of. They decided what information they needed and how to display it." Zuboff sees this experience almost in terms of an averted struggle for power: "A hole had been poked in the knowledge dam." The consequence of handing down information "that had been preserved for managerial use and that had bolstered the necessity of imperative control" was that initial predicted savings of $370,000 for the first year were handsomely exceeded: the actual tally was $456,000.

After eight months, however, the savings levelled off: one of its progenitors believed that another 70% of the system's potential was not being used – and the barriers mostly had to do with people's understanding of the system. The operators themselves blamed management: as Zuboff summarises the issue, "The managers felt threatened, they resisted, and finally they had tried to 'steal the thunder' from the operators. As a result, the operators began to withdraw their care and concern. They were not prepared to fight: they were not sure how."

Similar trials of strength are likely to be staged in office after office. David Harvey, an authority on executive information systems, writes that these have "profound implications for the relationships and responsibilities of managers in the corporate hierarchy. Unless these are handled with foresight and intelligence, a system can sour the whole management culture, as executives down the line suddenly discover that power derived from the custodial role over certain corporate information has been usurped electronically."

On the face of it, such situations are absurd. Would managers rebel against a system designed to improve senior decision-making because its contents threatened their own authority? In brutal fact, unless firm action is taken, the story of the expense tracking system can all too easily be repeated far higher up and with vastly greater sums at stake than a few hundred thousand dollars. It's a truism that in organisations, knowledge is power. The only way to prevent the truism from becoming a barrier to performance – stopping that final 70% of potential from being achieved – is to emulate Alexander the Great's attitude to the Gordian Knot.

He cut through the problem with a single stroke. That cut is to abolish the concept of "ownership" of information. In fact, the networks which are the sinews of the office revolution rest on this abolition of ownership. All the information in the network is available to all its users as the material for the common work. How far down the company the use extends is a matter for decision – although the probability is that the network will spread further and further down over time. For that, there is excellent reason – performance lower down the company will be enhanced if those using its systems are actively engaged in both their design and purpose as well as their operation.

The Unstructured Upheaval

Try to cut them off from participation, and you get, not only the alienation recorded in Zuboff's sketches, but inferior performance – not so much of the people as the system. Moreover, the efforts of the people to regain some degree of participation can have grave results. Zuboff records the tactics adopted by the expense tracking operators when "playing around" with the system "to get at its potential" was in effect outlawed by management: "operators designed the experiments to be conducted on the graveyard shift, from midnight to 6 a.m." when "they were free to 'play' and learn without managerial pressure".

Zuboff doesn't draw the analogy: but engineers playing around with the safety controls of a nuclear reactor in the small hours of the morning at Chernobyl almost created a graveyard, not just for that part of Russia, but for whole, wide tracts of Europe. The case is extreme: but neither knowledge-based systems nor the people who operate them are dumb. The task of management is not to bar operational employees – those in structured jobs – from exercising initiative and developing interest in their work, but to find out ways of exploiting the system's undoubted ability, not to isolate people, but to create opportunities for shared work.

Zuboff notes that, when the electronic displays indicated trouble in the control rooms, operators would form small *ad hoc* groups to discuss the fault and work out the correct reaction. These informal meetings lasted half to three-quarters of an hour, but are characteristic of the way in which the screen-based environment creates group working. Confining people to their work stations, sealed off by partitions (which are actually mythical barriers, since they are so easily looked over and round and dismantled), is a denial of the system's capabilities and a waste of much of the investment.

Worse still, it's literally an insult to the intelligence of those who operate the system. Their ability as individuals, and as individuals working in groups, to improve the results of the organisation rests in the use of the screens to strengthen other means of human communication – not to replace them. It's true that bottom-up communication sits uneasily with hierarchy and possessive attitudes to information and power. But the latter are unsuited, indeed inimical to the needs of unstructured work and competitive organisations in the modern age.

What's true of structured work must be doubly, trebly, quadruply true of unstructured tasks, those which are capable of adding by far the most value. Cases like those cited by Zuboff demonstrate that, so long as human beings are involved, even the structured tasks of order processing, purchasing, accounting, paying, stocking, calculating, etc will be performed better by the injection of the unstructured action of human creativity. The full benefit of the unstructured upheaval, both at this level and at the higher level of decision, can't be achieved within an organisational strait-jacket.

Consider rather a device that Leffingwell, the scientific office manager, didn't include in his paraphernalia: the suggestion box. As Edward de Bono has written, "People are no longer a pair of working hands. They must contribute with their minds as well. In Toyota the average number of suggestions per employee per year is 326." More than one idea per person per working day: it's the kind of resource that the office revolution will make readily available. Think of the entire corporate system as an electronic suggestion box – and the partitions, real and imagined, start to fall away.

Chapter 27

THE INFORMATION EXPLOSION

Much of Shoshana Zuboff's book, *In the Age of the Smart Machine,* is concerned with the tension between the new technology and the old authority of the manager. As she notes, more is at stake than the orderly internal conduct of the affairs of the firm. The managers she studied at three plants had begun "to see that dealing with the tidal wave of increased information in a timely and insightful way was likely to provide their most crucial source of comparative advantage ... technology [of their own processes] alone would not provide an enduring competitive edge."

She argued persuasively for "a redefinition of the system of authority" to avoid what had happened at a company nicknamed "Global Bank Brazil". In that organisation, resistance "to opening up knowledge and developing the skills with which to master information crippled the productive capacity of many organisational members at every level and hampered the bank's ability to fulfil its strategic ambitions".

Are knowledge and authority truly on a "collision course"? It's true that senior management, at first sight, seems to have been offered a choice between an open society and a transparent one. Zuboff's brilliant image for the latter is Jeremy Bentham's fantastical architectural notion, the Panopticon. This twelve-sided iron and glass polygon was to provide the governor in its central tower with a clear view of everybody in each of its cells – none of whom could see the central observer. The Panopticon was, of course, intended in the first instance for a prison – and Zuboff is quick to make the point.

"Information systems that translate, record, and display human behaviour," she writes, "can provide the computer age version of universal transparency with a degree of illumination that would have exceeded even Bentham's most outlandish fantasies." It's a curious twist of events that the philosopher whose sovereign idea was "the greatest good of the greatest possible number" should have partially fathered present-day systems which do little good to either the inmates or the administrators – not only in prisons, but in hospitals. The large hospital dormitories known in Britain as "Nightingale wards" after their Victorian progenitor rely, like any bullpen office of the same period, on the principle of universal visibility and supervision.

Office Systems Technology can be used in exactly the same way, only far more effectively. Not only can senior management review the achievements and plans of subordinates at the press of a button or two: it can in theory dig down into the malfunctioning of any part of the manufacturing or marketing process – and intervene, interfere, second-guess at will. This power, however, goes against the grain of the modern movement in managing people. As Zuboff remarks, nowadays "Managers are exhorted to revamp their methods of communication, invite feedback, give feedback, listen, coach, facilitate, manage by objectives, encourage autonomy, provide vision, *et cetera.*"

Just as the electronic Panopticon can theoretically provide total authoritarian control, so it can achieve precisely the opposite. The new system *is* a revamped method of communication, it *does* both invite and give feedback, it encourages listening, it can be used highly effectively as a coaching device, it's an enormously powerful facilitator, it encourages autonomy precisely because control and visibility are enhanced, while the use of cerebral powers such as Zuboff describes ("conceptual, informational, procedural and systemic") is the very stuff of vision.

The collision course, in other words, is not inevitable. One study of Nightingale wards points in the opposite direction. Far from providing more effective use of nursing staff and supervision of the patients, the wards prove less economical and effective than single rooms. Why? First, the great majority of patients in any hospital are quite fit enough to look after themselves, and are happier doing so: there's no need for constant supervision or nursing service. Second, periodic checks of patients who do need care and attention can be done perfectly well through windows or doors (or, still more effectively, via closed circuit TV). Third, the privacy of single rooms makes treatment, examination, crises, etc. much more easily manageable. Fourth, the large wards are inflexible and lead to uneconomic allocation of bed space.

Translate all this into the office culture and you get the basic principles of modern management.

1. Give people the authority they need to do their own jobs on their own initiative.
2. Manage by exception – intervene only when intervention is evidently called for.

3. Suit the environment and the organisation to the purpose – that is, for example, *ad hoc* groups rather than fixed departments.
4. Aim for LIMO at all times – least input for most output.

Once again, no more powerful means of accomplishing these four objectives with strength and safety combined has been devised than Office Systems Technology. Once again, though, the spirit in which the system is used determines its utility and its performance. Zuboff found "several executives" who "recognised the technology as an opportunity to increase conformity to management's expectations". In their narrow view, management by exception wouldn't be used as a liberating device but as a disciplinary rod: "As an organisation, we will be able to target the exceptions and work on where the pain is ... The information system will force awareness of exceptions down into the organisation."

What's more, the awareness would generate a "bloodless automaticity" of compliance and conformity. That is, of course, a fantasy every bit as weird as Jeremy Bentham's. The reality is that senior managers, far from getting automatic obedience, will be tempted to take too much on their shoulders as the information comes to their fingertips: "It is very hard for a top manager," said one, "to have information and not want to do something about it." In this scenario, top managers "steal" information from the subordinates and use it to subvert their authority, while the subordinates in consequence seek to "restrict or impede their superiors' access".

Zuboff sees this problem bearing hard on middle managers – those Drucker "relays" again – whose "role has been largely defined by the collection, analysis and dissemination of information". Now, the routine information goes through the system, not them: and their non-routine information obtained face-to-face has become less valuable, too. No doubt, this is true. But the whole argument is built around, and collapses about, the idea of management as static and singular. Substitute instead a dynamic, perceptive, multiple environment, and the hoarding of information becomes both counter-productive and self-defeating. How can you share in a solution if you won't contribute to the discussion of the problem?

How can you maintain a dynamic business without meeting change and challenge? And how can that be done in the absence of effective information? It's no coincidence that the information industry – newspapers, magazines, newsletters, agency services and every form of communicated word and film – has emerged as the world's fastest growing. At a time when change is impinging on management faster than ever before, the links between external information and the internal information in the network and the database have become vital, too.

Anyway, most of the information will already be there, on open file, on the screen. Another of Zuboff's examples, "Drug Corporation", gives the lie to the whole controversy. In successful research and development projects, "personal communication was the crucial factor in 80% of the cases". Formal resources ("publications, libraries or computerised data retrieval systems") contributed only 5% to 20% of the useful knowledge. Very intelligently, this company long ago (a dozen years before the nineties started) began to construct a computer-conferencing system with the sci-fi aim of creating a "universal mind" – one that "would span time and distance".

In a distinctly formal, hierarchical, carefully controlled corporate environment ("negotiations between divisions are made 'from the top down'"), the conferencing system, known as DIALOG, appears to have been a success, and the more informally used, the more successful. Few examples are given: but one researcher got a knotty software problem resolved in a few days through DIALOG, and density problems in making one ointment appear to have been solved far more rapidly than would otherwise have been possible. Perhaps of necessity, much of the evidence is subjective: one analyst said that the system led "to less arbitrary and single-minded decisions based on limited data".

Whether they were better decisions isn't recorded, though that must be the assumption. You don't have to make very large assumptions, however, to feel that the DIALOG process must be superior. First, there's no problem of getting all required participants in the same place at the same time. Second, nobody has to travel or alter their timetables. Third, the "thought-interactive" process extends over a week or two – decisions aren't rushed in an hour. Fourth, and above all, "Before you are called on, you have the opportunity to see what others have said, think about it, organise your thoughts and marshal your arguments."

That is an excellent description of the system in its managerial capacity: to provide vision, thought, organised and marshalled arguments. As noted in other chapters, the system has more immediately obvious benefits. It puts people on the same plane. They lose the inhibitions of rank, physical appearance or vocal fluency, but without losing the expressiveness of speech: capitals become the equivalent of a shout and the drug company even spawned a symbol ("7") for "tongue in cheek". However, the system's role in creating peers can be exaggerated, because most of the R & D people concerned actually *were* peers.

When DIALOG was transferred from R & D, and managers were added, the inequalities apparently made computer conferencing less useful. Knowing that a contribution came from a superior, subordinates might even take it as an order. In a hierarchical company like Drug Corporation, it will take time for people at both ends of the order-and-obey chain to get used to give and take. "Managers will act on beliefs," one professional told Zuboff, "as though they were truths rather than accept the paralysis of being uncertain." But ambiguity is the essence of management in changing, competitive times – in which informality, too, is essential.

Drug Corporation was the scene of perhaps the greatest possible effort at informality, a "Computer Coffee Break", based on the undoubtedly true notion that people need breaks and humour in their working lives to stimulate creativity and improve morale. Only members could "read" that text; but it "quickly became the most popular conference in DIALOG". The trouble was that, as its uninhibited use came to the attention of senior managers, many didn't like what they saw – not at all. Free, open and informal communication was one thing: dirty stories and attacks on management over the network were another.

The result was highly predictable: the electronic coffee break was killed. Drug Corporation, however, continued to use conferencing, although in a new and more structured system called Total Office Network Integration – or TONI. While this represented in some respects a deliberate attempt to turn back the tide, there were two highly significant riders. First, the new strictness was hardly consistent with "the free flow and creative use of information" which "mounting competitive pressures" demanded. Second, setting up such systems lets a genie out of the bottle: Zuboff's account is full of phrases from her subjects like "an irreversible trend", "autonomous power", "the system is moving on its own".

The trend, the power and the movement are away from the classic situation in which managers require employees; in which superiors have subordinates; jobs are defined to be specific, detailed, narrow and task-related; and organisations have levels that in turn make possible chains of command and spans of control. To put this issue in a phrase, you cannot place unstructured work in a structured straitjacket. In searching for an analogy, to set against "the two-class system marked by an insurmountable gulf between workers and managers", Zuboff suggests the trajectory of a professional career. But there's a more fruitful metaphor in another observation - that the new technology has created a learning imperative.

Several thinkers, including Peter Drucker, have put forward the necessity of the company becoming a learning organisation. Could its management therefore come to resemble that of a school? Information is learning: you turn to the system, as to textbooks, or libraries, to discover the data (or learn things) that you didn't know. You do so both as an individual (student) and in groups (classes), in which the good teacher leads, but does not dictate. You don't in the early stages of a scholastic career concentrate on one narrow discipline, but acquire a wide competence, based always on learning.

Moreover, you demonstrate competence in learning by its application – by your "results". The results lead to your advance into progressively more closely defined, but more important and senior work. At all times, you are encouraged to show originality and independence of thought (from which the best results follow), but without ever being allowed to forget the importance of basic disciplines – including the discipline of organisation itself. The most senior students, indeed, take over this responsibility of maintaining the rules, and revising them regularly, so that the organisation can meet its overriding objective.

While there is thus a hierarchy of discipline, there is no hierarchy of information. Anybody can get access to any learning they need, and many different forums are maintained and encouraged so that information can be freely exchanged and debated. The founders of the electronic coffee break had half of a good idea: had the informal cross-chat been confined within the formal purposes of the organisation, it would have helped to forward the development of the drug company's open office system, instead of retarding it.

English schools have the word "monitor" to describe senior pupils who exercise delegated authority over their fellow students. Managerial authority will increasingly mean the creative monitoring of unstructured work that will flow mainly through and round the computer-based system. Tension will only arise where one side or the other departs from shared views of what the monitoring is designed to achieve: and that can be defined as self-disciplined success for the individual manager and thus collective success for the learning organisation to which he or she belongs.

Chapter 28

THE WHOLE CORPORATION

The ideas in this book have been strongly influenced by the work carried out at the Palo Alto Research Center of Xerox Corporation. That's hardly surprising, given that, to quote *Business Week*, the "now-famous" centre's "vision of the electronic office was so advanced that fifteen years later its early efforts still influence computer design". Workstations from Sun Microsystems and Apollo Computer, the Apple Macintosh and its mouse, and Microsoft's Windows programs for PCs – all have roots in PARC and the graphical user interface which it pioneered.

Without question, its researchers have shown equal vision in discerning the coming shape of the office. Yet at the start of the 1990s, no corporation (including Xerox itself) had succeeded in creating a strong, profitable market in selling office systems of the type described in these pages and identified as the dominant life-form of the next century's corporations. In the spring of 1990, the story would have been little different from that of 1989, when a dedicated advocate of the new order could state flatly that "the integrated work station hardly exists".

At that date, in the United States, Xerox had changed to a more targeted strategy: "in selling customised systems to selected industries," reported that same issue of *Business Week*, "it will pick and choose gear from a variety of other suppliers." The reporter had plainly not fully gathered the significance of the unfolding revolution (document-processing workstations were described as "essentially fancy personal computers", which misses the point by several miles). But there's no denying that the actual commercial results for suppliers have yet to match either the gains won by the first pioneering users or the brilliance of the technological promise.

Take what will happen if and when (it will surely be "when") the dot-by-dot electronic technology of digital copying takes over. "That way," says the same magazine, "a single machine might scan text and

195

pictures, and store, fax or send them to other machines on a network – plus make paper copies. Such a 'smart' copier – essentially a computer – might also drive terminals throughout an office." In other words, this road, too, leads to Rome, to the goal of an integrated office in which technology plays the role of integrating, not only all office systems, but all those who use them.

The question remains: why is this a goal, not a thriving market? There are identifiable practical problems: terminals and personal computers that are hard to use and restrictive in the language they employ; difficulties in going beyond data to the illustrative use of pictures and graphics which enhances the cognitive power of the system; lack of access to other systems through the absence of networking.

This book has made it clear that these problems can either be overcome right now or will cease to exist on a very short timescale. The bigger problems by far are psychological and organisational – the same kind of hang-ups that led Xerox itself to underexploit the pioneering of PARC (today, significantly, its research is "being plugged into corporate strategic planning" to ensure that there will be no repetition of that error). PARC's very wide-ranging brief, when it began its research into the office, was to look twenty years into the future to find out what different requirements would arise.

Its findings challenged, not just the basis of the historic office, but the foundations of prevailing management practice. Much lip-service has been lavished on delegation and devolution of power to discrete business units. But the spirit of monolithic, hierarchical, functional management still hovers over the waters. None of these attributes is suitable for a rapidly changing, competitive environment: nor, for that matter, is wholesale decentralisation. Increasingly, as Rank Xerox (UK) Ltd's managing director, David O'Brien, puts it, "How you play your strengths across the board is what counts."

If you can "bring the whole together", it can "become what is to all intents and purposes one independent business at the point of impact, bringing to bear critical mass, critical strengths and critical skills". That point of impact is the market. The company has to become both market-led and market-leading, both responding to and anticipating the evolution in customer requirements. But that can't be achieved simply by investing in Office Systems Technology. It requires a far more difficult commitment, in O'Brien's words, to accepting "the dynamics of the environment and the need for constant cultural change".

Since that may well mean a new executive team (as it did at both RXL and its Xerox parent in the 1980s), you can easily understand managerial reluctance to enter the new era. The organisational norms, as RXL found, can only be cracked by a major education and training effort, a major rethinking of management philosophy, and an attack on obsolete elements in the corporate culture. Otherwise, the company can't move to the thinking, creative, team-oriented management that O'Brien calls "holistic" or, more vividly "whole-istic".

Wholeness doesn't only refer to integration of subsidiaries, but to that of production, marketing, design, sales, finance, personnel – all the resources which are far stronger together and far weaker apart. The manager of tomorrow must be highly skilled in the specialism of the moment, but also broadly versed across the whole spectrum of the business, performance-oriented, able and eager to take responsibility, deeply informed in specific markets ... it's a daunting catalogue; but in a dynamic environment, the general manager has no choice but to be both marketer and finance director, personnel director and product developer, manufacturing director and salesperson, expert in public relations and in planning.

The specialist professionals, for their part, can't exercise their own specialities effectively save in the same multi-faceted context. The multi-channel, multi-user, multi-media network is the technological means to the organisational end of integrating information and its use for the purposes of the multifarious manager.

In the unfolding era, managers have a great advantage over their predecessors: now managers control the system – they call the shots. As this investigation has shown, the shots can be called wrongly. It doesn't follow that a more open, collegiate and genuinely interactive society will emerge at the top. But efforts to use Office Systems Technology to reinforce hierarchy, rather than supplant it, will fail in the court from which, these days, there is no appeal – the market-place.

The fate of commercial dictatorships will then be no different from that of the managerial ostriches who, even if they sense that the office is changing in a revolutionary style, rest on the killing prayer "Not yet". Procrastination is bad for them, their companies and their other office workers, for whom the new technology holds out a new prospect – a future in which the work may come to them at least as often as they must go to the work: in which dull routine is automated, and interesting, unstructured tasks are enhanced by the ability to interact with others in genuine group working.

If that sounds Utopian, that is merely a consequence of the fact that the information-based office actually does provide leaps forward comparable to that from the horse and buggy to the automobile – not the Model T, either, but the latest model. Perhaps the metaphor is too shallow, for in terms of moving from A to B, the efficiency gain since

Henry Ford has not been phenomenal. A better analogy is the jet age, which in revolutionising travel also made possible the global business.

The electronic age will have a similar impact on the nature of the management process. Studies cited by Rank Xerox indicate that 20% of management time is spent gathering information (data management), and another fifth on communicating conclusions ("composition" management). The 60% in the middle divides roughly equally between housekeeping (or organising), meetings and thinking – thus, only 20% of time is spent on moving the business forward: and the last figure may be a significant exaggeration for many managers.

To quote O'Brien, "In some organisations there is almost no thinking at all." As managers spend all their time managing the process, the rules and the policies, "the organisation sinks to a mode of operation called 'ludicy' – playing the game for the game's sake, not the achievement of goals". Technology's impact, for managers who want to play the right game, is to improve data management in cost, time and accuracy; to reduce both housekeeping and meetings in frequency, cost and time, leaving more time to improve the quality of thinking; and to improve communication in cost, time and timeliness, or "currency". The improvements can be expressed in a halving of the time expended on each count. On this model, then, 60% of managerial time is freed for interacting with others – exchanging views and opinions, developing ideas and enhancing understanding.

How realistic is this threefold gain? The findings reflect PARC's fundamental research, which established the AUC model of office work – standing for Acquire, Understand and Communicate. In the "acquisition" mode, the advantages of having widely dispersed information sources brought together into one work station, and paper text replaced by electronics, are self-evident. "Acquisition" is the "communication" mode in reverse, and the advantages are identical for both. Information moves faster and more accurately, and the time-lags are minimal.

Many examples in this book have demonstrated these so-to-speak mechanical benefits of the electronic office in the Acquire and Communicate phases. To the extent that managers should spend the least possible time on mechanical functions, and the most on intellectual activity, the latter automatically gains. Managers will need to resist the temptation to acquire more and more information, or send more and more messages, simply because of the ease and speed, and that will be no easier than exercising reasonable time discipline in the office of the past. But even if there were no Acquire and Communicate benefits in time (unlikely), the other gains (cost, accuracy and currency) are more rather than less important.

Moreover, considerable Understand benefits would still be available in theory – a doubling of thinking time, savings in cost, plus improvement in quality. Whether theory equates with practice depends on some highly objective judgments. You can see without difficulty how an electronic desktop that tidies itself up, manipulates files and documents, swiftly searches for missing items, and so on could halve the time spent on housekeeping. One look at some executive desks, festooned with papers in untidy piles, is enough to make the point.

That about meetings takes more argument. O'Brien's case is that more effective communication via the screens will exchange views and opinions that would conventionally involve people coming face-to-face – the network thus "eliminates meetings that just keep everyone in touch, or debate where we are relative to where we should be, ending in arguments due to misunderstanding or inconsistent data". It takes no great faith to believe that members of groups who are in constant, documented contact will require many fewer contact meetings; nor that the superior preparation made possible by the system will obtain better results in faster time than the conventional meeting – which, moreover, cannot "play" with the data to help in its decisions.

Nor can the screenless individual manager. The argument that the quality of his output will improve is based on the increased time available for the constructive, thinking phase; the interaction with other managers in genuine cross-functional group working which is facilitated by the network; and the availability of better data-processing and data-gathering supports at the electronic desk. Its document-based architecture (as opposed to the data-based architecture which still dominated most hardware supplied to offices as the 1980s ended) is analogous to the management process, and must enhance that process in the hands of converted managers.

As with all revolutions, the outcome will turn on the pace of conversion. O'Brien is plainly right to say that the quality of management is the fundamental issue. There is a potential Catch 22 here: the electronic office produces high-quality management, but it takes high-quality management to install the electronic office. Such circuits, however, can be broken by external intervention. The pressures building up beneath conservative managements from both competitive forces and the changing nature of the workforce must ultimately prove irresistible. For the late-comers, the new technology will offer the only escape route. For those who are first to enter this new world, the quantifiable benefits will be their cost justification: the qualitative benefit will be their true payback.

Chapter 29

THE CORPORATION OF THE FUTURE

The history of management thought in the post-war era can be compressed into three words: coping with scale. As markets have expanded, businesses have inevitably enlarged, until today's middling company is the size of yesterday's giant, and today's small firm would have been a significant medium-sized company in the fifties. Markets have not only expanded in volume: they have proliferated in variety, and spread geographically. As this unstoppable growth has gathered momentum, so the nature of the corporation has ineluctably changed.

The concerns of a multi-national, multi-product, multi-market, multifarious company are very different in order and complexity from those of a simple, homogenous business. When centralisation proved unable to cope with this massive step-change, centrally imposed decentralisation was attempted. When that failed in turn, matrix organisation was devised to combine, it was hoped, the virtues of decentralisation and centralisation. When that proved too cumbersome for comfort, devolution to market-oriented business units took over as the theoretically dominant mode.

Throughout the process, far-sighted business thinkers and leaders foresaw that the current solutions wouldn't work, and that a new concept of the corporation was required. Peter C. McColough, a decisive influence in the growth of the Xerox Corporation, which created one of the great post-war new technology surges, stands out as one such management visionary. His interview in the *Harvard Business Review* (May-June 1975) on "The Corporation and its Obligations" is a celebrated landmark in the evolution of modern thought on corporate social and political responsibilities.

McColough brought the same quality of vision to the internal development of the corporation. Five years before the *HBR* interview, in March 1970, McColough addressed the New York Society of Security Analysts on "Searching For An Architecture of Information". He noted that "Knowledge has already been projected as an industry in its own right, wrapped in the assurances of endless growth and self-renewing opportunity". He talked of the "knowledge explosion" being easily seen as a "supreme tool", but warned that it could also be viewed as a "potential tyrant".

McColough told his audience about a "hard reality . . . in attempting to gather, process, absorb, and disseminate information and knowledge, we find ourselves living more and more in the confusion of tied-up telephones, computer printout, procedure manuals, stacked airplanes, unnecessary correspondence, meetings, mail, memoranda and aging files marked 'Must Read' ". The basic purpose of his own corporation was "to find the best means to bring greater order and discipline to information". The phrase "the architecture of information", coined in this address, was pregnant with the future: McColough foresaw correctly that information would interact with work to change corporate life for the better.

"What we seek", he said, "is to think of information itself as a natural and undeveloped environment which can be enclosed and made more habitable for the people who live and work within it". But in 1970 office visionaries lacked the practical tools to turn their dreams into reality. McColough thought that the office of 1980 would be radically different from that of the time when he spoke. In that he was all too optimistic. Within six years of his speech, true, the scientists and engineers at the Palo Alto Research Corporation, which he had established in pursuit of his vision, had brilliantly resolved the basic technical problems. But the organisational ones stayed.

The typical corporation of the Eighties remained inflexible, hard to move from the centre, and impossible to budge from the periphery, even though the necessary means of action, interaction, control and response – tools which McColough could only foresee – were becoming more and more available. In many respects the office world of 1990 (and never mind 1980) still stood aloof from the "architecture of information", which, like all revolutionary concepts, has had to wait for revolutionary times.

Over the years since 1970 the means of management have necessarily improved as the scale of need has mounted. But the leaps forward in communications, and the universal, enormous spread in computerisation of structured work, have always lagged appreciably behind that need. Towards the end of the eighties, however, the situation was dramatically reversed. The technology began not only to speed past the current requirement, but to race beyond the ability of current managers to grasp the significance of the new means of management and to put this vast potential to profitable work.

The consequent fumblings have made many large corporations look so clumsy as to raise a literally large question: is bigness finished? No longer does anybody believe the conventional wisdom of the sixties, which held that no more than 300 multi-national giants would inherit the commercial earth. This view, seizing on the thoughts of a Swiss-based professor (that small nation's own success in a superpower world should have given him pause), was still strong enough in the eighties to inspire even an advertising agency with dreams of world dominion. This was Saatchi & Saatchi, drawing its inspiration from one of the post-war period's best-known management thinkers, Theodore J. Levitt.

Later editor of the admirable *Harvard Business Review*, Levitt first won fame for the "marketing myopia" thesis, which argued primarily that inadequate, short-sighted response to technological change was the root cause of strategic failure. However, his corollary, that companies should define and if necessary redefine their businesses (to ensure that they took the right technological path), attracted far greater attention. As the author himself has written, in a remarkably frank account, this thesis was seized by managements as an excuse for aggrandisement by all manner of inappropriate diversification.

With equal candour, Levitt has identified the weaknesses in his arguments in favour of global marketing which so impressed Saatchis. This view fleshed out the 300-giant thesis by enumerating the economic advantages which global corporations marketing global products globally would inevitably gain over their lesser brethren: presumably, national companies marketing national products nationally. As it happened, however, Saatchis itself fell victim to the central weakness of the theory: which is that the whole is certainly no stronger than its parts, and may be weaker.

That's because the need to exert control (for a global business that is not globally co-ordinated doesn't deserve its name) may both outrun the reach of central management and stultify the ambitions and energies of local companies. Moreover, the stock market value of conglomerates tends to fall below the separate value of their parts. At that point, they are theoretically vulnerable to takeover and break-up. In the seventies and eighties, theory became grim reality as some of the world's largest multi-nationals found themselves – astonishingly enough – on the receiving end of serious bids.

It could be argued that to be safe, the giants merely had to "stick to their knitting" – in contrast to heavily diversified tobacco giants like RJR Nabisco or BAT Industries, or to Saatchis, which broadened from advertising into marketing services and management consultancy. A laudable example of sticking to the global knitting would be IBM. If any mammoth supported the global thesis, this was the one.

The Corporation of the Future

Before anybody even dreamt of preaching globalism, IBM was selling the same product line in the same way in every market in the world, bound together by common global standards of corporate design, personnel policies and conduct, uniting strong national marketing and manufacturing companies by a global matrix organisation of great sophistication. Without question, IBM has been a unique powerhouse in its markets and the world economy. Yet in October 1989, the *Financial Times* had this to say:

> Indeed, the once invincible IBM today looks open to some of the more telling criticisms levelled at Britain's BAT.... Each company is built around a business (mainframe computers and tobacco) which is immensely profitable and generates huge amounts of cash. But both businesses are also mature, with unexciting growth prospects ... IBM has sought to diversify within the electronics industry but, like BAT, it has had limited success in finding new returns comparable to those on its core business.

The writer, Guy de Jonquières, pointed to IBM's "expensive flop" in telecommunications, where a disastrous acquisition, that of Rolm, was later resold to Siemens of West Germany, and to a fundamentally important fact: that the giant "is a weak contender in many fast-growing niche computer markets, such as lap-tops and work stations". This giant's experience is important testimony to the fact that, in a situation where markets are fragmenting and segmenting, in response to customer and technological pressures, the market power of any one company, however large, is inevitably threatened.

The larger the giant, indeed, the greater its problems: because fighting on so many fronts works against the effort to achieve co-ordinated success. Instead of battling a few competitors on a single front (an accurate description of the now-dead mainframe era which IBM dominated so absolutely), the giant must contend with many competitors in many different circumstances. IBM's experience is only typical of the general outcome: even its "legendary control over industry standards is now being challenged by smaller microelectronics and software firms, which have increasingly seized the initiative in product innovation".

It's instructive to recall, as de Jonquières does, that IBM's size was once the target of a long-drawn-out anti-trust action, brought by the Johnson Administration; the case was dropped under Reagan, when the company's grandeur was deemed necessary to the American economy in the context of global competition. IBM's subsequent surge of released power, notably in personal computers, must have looked ominous to smaller competitors. But the surge rapidly expired, for "If anything, the company's size has proven one of its biggest handicaps, saddling it with high costs and impeding its speed of market response."

What's sauce for IBM is surely sauce for other very large companies. Their loss of relative power can easily be exaggerated: in 1988 IBM's *profits* came to half the total *sales* of the runner-up in computers, Digital Equipment. It could hardly be described as vulnerable – although de Jonquières muses that "its market capitalisation of almost $60 billion *probably* [my italics] puts it beyond reach of a hostile bid." Most of its competitors would dearly love the company's market share even where (as in workstations) it is weak, and even where it has suffered amazing relative decline (personal computers).

In most Western markets, in fact, the giants of American and European business, despite the Japanese onslaught, still occupy the major stretches of territory. Their size still gives them access to immense cash flows and universal distribution. Even if they were to crumble collectively, their intact shares of individual markets would be inherited by others and would be central factors in the strategy of competitors and the course of markets. But the weight of money and market leadership is no longer automatically decisive. That is because:

1. Technology is developing too rapidly, across too broad a front, and in too many unpredictable directions for any one corporation to command all the technological heights.
2. Markets, as noted above, have fragmented in response to changing technology and segmenting customer demands, so that formerly monolithic markets, which monolithic companies could dominate, have split into large, specialised sectors, or "niches".
3. Ready availability of global finance has enabled new global ventures to develop from start-up to multi-billion dollar sales with unprecedented speed – and in direct competition with giants.
4. Large businesses no longer have a monopoly over the most efficient technology of manufacturing, distribution, and structured office work, because the IT revolution has brought optimum efficiency within the economic reach of all.

World domination by 300 companies was predicated on the theory that their possession of all the best technology, overwhelming financial resources, dominating shares of all markets and decisive economies of scale would prove to be insurmountable barriers to would-be stormers of the citadel. Not only that: but from within the citadel (like the Empire's forces in *Star Wars*), its defenders would easily snuff out

204

attacks when they had hardly begun. This mirror of impregnability has been shattered by the four factors listed above: if not in the hands of Western competitors, in those of Japanese firms – many of which were very far from giant-sized when their assaults began.

But the loss of technological, financial, market and managerial monopolies doesn't "finish" bigness. As events in the world car market of the late eighties showed, only small firms which act and think big can contend indefinitely with already large companies which have more money, more technology, more markets and more management resources. The paradox for the larger corporation, though, is that, to exploit these advantages, it must behave exactly like the dynamic smaller competitors that have sprung to market power in the segmented niches – many of which now contain billions of dollars in annual sales.

Leading managements are trying hard to achieve this arduous transformation. At United Technologies, for example, chief executive Bob Daniell is striving to "flatten the hierarchy", "empower his workers", and "get close to his customers" – all phrases that delineate classic differences between the large firm and the small. Because, as just noted, the transformation task is so arduous, Daniell, writes *Business Week*, "uses training to revamp the corporate culture. More than 5,000 senior and middle managers are getting at least 40 hours of classroom work." The headline reads "Train, train, train".

The story makes no mention of information technology's role in achieving what it calls "1990s-style management" at United Technologies. But the specific improvements cited are grist to the mill of Office Systems Technology. For instance, a request for a design improvement formerly required approval by nine departments and consumed "mountains of paper". Now, the engineer on the spot takes the decision and needs only three signatures before proceeding: average response time has dwindled from eighty-two days to ten, and the backlog is down to under a hundred cases: it once stood at 1,900.

To improve service, which was emerging as the Achilles' heel of the crucial Pratt & Whitney jet engine division, steps were taken like allowing field representatives to authorise warranty replacements involving several millions of dollars without waiting for headquarters approval. As previous chapters have demonstrated, elimination of paperwork and committees, and devolving information and authority to the sharp end, are essential elements in the improved quality of management which the office revolution can achieve – while strengthening, rather than weakening, control.

The alchemist's stone of management will never be found: perfect control combined with perfect delegation. Running a business continually involves trade-offs. Thus, companies need to change continuously and at increasing speed; but in turbulent times, they also require stability more than ever before. Powerful managers with freedom to decide are essential at all levels, but that doesn't lessen the demand for strong, creative leadership at the very top – or remove the evident possibility of tension between the levels. Then, innovation thrives on an element of anarchy, but implementation will fail without discipline. And managers must be free to criticise their nominal superiors, and to prevail against them in argument, but respect for superiors is part of the organisational cement ... and so on.

The "holistic" company doesn't ignore these conflicts: it simply regards their resolution as an ebb and flow that must be harnessed to produce excellent results. "Holism" is a Greek derivation that came late into English usage – in 1926, from the unlikely pen of the South African leader, Field Marshal J. C. Smuts. It refers, according to the *Shorter Oxford Dictionary*, to "The tendency in nature to produce wholes from the ordered grouping of units". In the holistic corporation, this tendency is a form of continuous mutation – the principle on which nature is founded.

In the economy of the twenty-first century, new large companies will coalesce and then sub-divide, mimicking nature, both internally and externally, only for the process to begin all over again. Inside the company, the grouping of units and the units themselves will mutate according to circumstances. To change the metaphor, and to return to one used earlier in this book, the managerial jazz group will change its members from time to time, and very possibly change its style. But for all this mutation to happen constructively and coherently, a single principle must apply all the time: obtaining a one-company, concentrated focus in every part of the business, every unit of holism.

Information is the genetic material of this process and this principle. In practical terms, the trends of the 1990s – such as the flatter hierarchies, decision-making pushed down the corporation and closeness to customers pursued by United Technologies among many others – all demand the circulation and availability of shared information. The office revolution takes what was almost impossibly difficult and transforms the near-impossible into a relatively simple management system, whose hardware and software components will be available off the shelf. But making the best use of that system will be anything but simple, for its users will be juggling with complex variables in a kaleidoscopic environment.

To become a successful juggler, "train, train, train" is indeed the only way. Another metaphor used in this book is that of the school – the learning organisation whose members have personal responsibility for what they learn and how they use their learning, who get individual recognition for their individual achievements, but whose own purposes are also those of the organisation. This is almost another definition of holism. Information technology in this context becomes education technology: the process of gathering and manipulating shared information in concert with others to achieve planned results is inevitably a learning process.

It is also good business. The downfall of large corporations begins when their traditional cycle – success, stagnation, crisis, rebirth, success, stagnation – starts to peak at successively lower levels. In 1963 the same Peter McColough, addressing an internal "Talk Leadership Seminar", asked an arresting question: "Is it inevitable that such organisations as Xerox should have their periods of emergence, full flower of growth and prestige and then later stagnation and death?"

He tracked the development from a "new organisation", like the early Xerox, which is "loose on procedure, unclear on organisational lines, variable in policies", to the mature company which, beset by written and unwritten rules and the "heavy hand of custom", becomes "less venturesome" as it accumulates "possessions, stature and reputation". McColough thought that "one of our greatest obstacles for future growth and vitality is that our people will not feel that they are in the know" and "therefore will become inert and ineffective". Making a powerful case for creativity, "trying new things and risking failure" and "inevitable mistakes", McColough delivered a grave warning – "that the only stability possible today is stability in motion".

Since his day, the Japanese have shown that the cycle of corporate stagnation is not built into human nature, but is the consequence of the defective organisation that leads to and institutionalises resistance to change. That stance has become impossible to maintain: but, thanks to the office revolution, mastery of change is now eminently possible, both for small businesses which want to be strong, and strong companies wise enough to seek the strengths of the small – to combine maturity, in the best sense of the word, with the freedom of movement, the "venturesome" enterprise and the "innovating, versatile and self-renewing men and women" that had created McColough's corporation of 1963, and that still provide the only paths to "continued vitality and progress".

Chapter 30

THE PERMANENCE OF CHANGE

In October 1944, *Fortune* magazine published an interesting paragraph on the latest innovation in the technology of the office. It ran as follows:

> A pen on an altogether different principle has been invented by the Hungarian journalist L. J. Biro, now in Argentina. Biro's pen uses a gelatinous ink of which it can hold a six months' supply. Since it is not a liquid, this ink can't leak. It is rolled, not poured, on paper by a ball bearing, almost one millimeter in diameter. This ball bearing is the pen's "point". It writes smoothly but thickly, like crayon. Parker says it does not fear the new pen. According to the company, some such device appears every few months to disappear soon after.

Men fear change as children fear to go in the dark. This re-working of Francis Bacon expresses a puzzling truth – because change is not only as inevitable as death, but embodies the potential for individual and social progress. The late British journalist Patrick Hutber made great satirical play with his "Law", holding that "better is worse". True, you cannot write copperplate script with a ballpoint pen: but much about Biro's innovation was truly better. When organisational change does mean decay, the deterioration is not generic, but results from poor management. In an overwhelming majority of cases, "worse" results from failure to change radically – through the kneejerk reaction which (*vide* Parker Pen) is called "industry experience", or the fear which goes under the name of conservatism.

Consequent disasters abound in politics (the Labour Party's long years of refusal to adapt to the consumer society), technology (RCA's failure to move from thermionic valves to transistors), economics (the Soviet Union's clinging to obsolete systems of allocating and utilising resources), and business strategy (the British car industry's long years of ignoring the need for an international, integrated product line). But in the world of information technology, resistance to change has been especially lethal, and the fatalities are coming faster as the pace of change accelerates.

Parker Pen had ample time to correct its error and become itself a maker of ballpoint pens (though a minor one, note). Today, the conservative have run out of time. The preface to this book emphasised the soaring rise in the power of personal computers, measured in millions of instructions per second (mips). But the sinking cost is no less fantastic. Between 1989 and 1995, according to the Gartner Group, the hardware cost of one million instructions per second for a mainframe purchaser will fall from $116,786 to $39,490. For a mini buyer, the cost, $10,975 in 1989, will decline to an astonishing $738. But even that low figure will still be *double* the 1989 cost of a single mips for a desktop machine. Far more fantastic still, the mini's cost per mips will be *forty-three* times the desktop equivalent in 1995.

Plainly, the technological wave producing these amazing, fundamental and irreversible changes in economic relationships cannot be withstood. The mainframes and the minis certainly have a future. But that, in the words of *Business Week*, is "as the communications switches and storehouses for networks of desktops". In other words, the master has become the servant, and the servant the master. To argue about the desirability of this change is peculiarly futile: it has already happened, in the sense that the technological express is thundering along inevitably towards this destination.

The issue is not whether change can be delayed (for it cannot be), still less whether it can be prevented, but how best to exploit its opportunities. In a static world, chances are few: although that statement is truly meaningless, because the world has never stood still, and never can. The office revolution, though, is one of the rare high-order changes that is both problem and solution rolled into one. The problem arises from the fact that Office Systems Technology cannot be installed with full effect unless the company radically alters its management methodology. The solution arises from the fact that OST itself forces and facilitates the necessary changes in management.

The examples can be quite humdrum, like the savings made by a professional practice whose consultants no longer draft their reports in longhand for transcribing by secretaries: instead, the drafts are typed straight into the system. Or the uses can be relatively advanced, like the reduction in meeting time produced by preliminary interactive discussion – so that the meeting is not a forum for argument over the facts. With these agreed, the meeting can genuinely evaluate the alternatives and come to a genuine consensus.

The real issue is the change from using information technology as a quantitative tool to adopting its powers as a qualitative weapon. The difference is well expressed in an article by Dr Robert Shaw for *Finance* magazine on the application of IT to marketing. So far, he observes, the applications of IT have mostly been quantitative in effect: automation has improved salesforce productivity – for instance, by making it unnecessary for people to return to the office to make their sales reports, or to discover vital information about prices, delivery or technical information. But firms are also increasingly using their IT power qualitatively, to construct databases that identify "the needs and behaviour of both existing and prospective customers".

Fusion of the two, Shaw writes, greatly augments the qualitative effect, signalling "a new move in the age-old game of knowing the customer". The computer-based concept of "database marketing, lifestyle marketing or targeted marketing", he believes, will lift information technology "into the front line of marketing strategy formulation". And yet he also reports surveys "which show that marketers are being both slow and unimaginative in their use of information technology equipment and programs".

Major costs are at stake – for example, it costs £100,000 a year to keep a salesman on the road, while an average of more than six calls is required to clinch an order (up from four in 1979). Anything that can improve the quality and quantity of the marketing effort would surely be manna from heaven to hard-pressed marketers. Human nature, however, distrusts manna, whether it comes from heaven or from management gurus or from IT suppliers. The conservative, costly bird in the hand is preferred to the two birds in the bush of change and cost-effectiveness.

Through exactly the same working of psychological forces, highly astute, experienced and battle-hardened chief executives can fail to take elementary precautions against highly feasible events – such as currency fluctuations or overstated profits in an acquisition target. They do so, what's more, in full knowledge of the wise alternative – which is probably also true of most of the marketers mentioned above. Managers seldom commit sins of omission or commission of which the organisation is wholly ignorant.

Ignorance in this sense doesn't explain ignorance in the other: when, say, large and sophisticated multi-nationals have divisions which don't know their profits by customer or by product, or are making no investment or investigation into PC-based networks or information systems. Somebody in the organisation has heard of these analyses and these systems and their power. Yet managers who learn of such mysteries at the feet of some guru too rarely insist on putting their new learning into practice – even though they are intellectually convinced of its compelling strength.

There is a common thread to all such invited ignorance. Doing nothing appears less risky than promoting change, which by definition involves making many new decisions: they in turn have to be based on uncertain and therefore potentially dangerous assumptions. The proposed change may promise positive and large benefits in the future: but it also incurs much *negative* reward – drawbacks, risks and disadvantages which operate strongly in the here and now. The positive rewards may arrive in the longer term: on the other hand, they may not.

Faced with an excess of immediate negatives over no or uncertain positives, people from chief executives downwards take the easy option. For the manager who doesn't change, that means no option at all. That, of course, also involves making assumptions, which are no less dangerous for being implicit. But unlike new initiatives, standing pat doesn't involve new endeavour. Suppose that one of Dr Shaw's marketing companies becomes really serious about getting "close to the customer" or "total quality management" (which are two sides of the same coin). What will the consequences be?

In most industrial companies, few people ever see real, live customers. They are mostly left to the distributors. Impaling all managers on the really sharp end will pay off positively and grandly – but what about the negative rewards of the inevitable upheaval? Breaking down barriers between departments, stopping dependence on inspection to achieve quality, and ceasing to award business on price alone, again, are all far easier said than done. But without them (and eleven other equally fierce stipulations) organisations can't come within bargepole distance of the W. Edwards Deming approach to quality that has so inspired the Japanese. But there's more than inertia to blame.

Every management is faced with multiple options multiplied by many facets of the corporation to produce an infinite number of tasks. But every management only has a strictly finite amount of time and energy. There has to be an order of priorities, which, all too often, is determined by events rather than needs. The wrong priority – say, an unsuccessful takeover bid – will be massively expensive in cash terms. But the sums won't include the totally hidden opportunity cost: that of what might have been created had the chief executive spent his time, say, on saving time.

As an earlier chapter pointed out, reducing the period spent between receipt and filling of customer orders is the latest Japanese-inspired source of "competitive advantage". But priorities won't be ordered and achieved better unless senior managers save their own time by effective delegation of priority tasks to colleagues with whom they keep in communion by modern technology. The executive information system and the networked personal computer offer chief executives and their organisations the ability to optimise the resolutions of all the conflicts listed above.

The office revolution will greatly improve the availability and timeliness of internal and external information – including relevant advances in the technology of product and process. It will immensely increase the ability to test assumptions for their soundness. It will vastly assist the ordering of priorities and, by speeding up the management process, leave senior management with fewer "either-or" choices of priority (one or the other, but not both). Total quality management can't be achieved without effective information systems; nor can closeness to the customer: with good systems, both can be built into the corporate routine.

Above all, Office Systems Technology will more readily expose the cost of resistance to change and will help overcome conservatism by building efficient unstructured responses into the management process through expert systems – so that foreign exchange fiascos, for example, are relegated to antiquity. All the above, moreover, will hinge on the system's ability to enable delegation without degradation of management quality – because the quality of management is both facilitated and supervised through the system.

Unfortunately, both the devolution of power and the wholehearted adoption of IT involve change, and fairly dramatic change, at that – especially for middle-aged managers who regard keyboards with dark distrust. But this is a problem of transition only. The ultimate folly of conservatism is that it is doomed. Take the examples given at the start of this chapter – and not just that of the ballpoint pen.

The Labour Party eventually gave way to the consumer society, in a flurry of red roses and marketing ploys ... but not until its obduracy had given the Conservatives over a decade of Thatcherite power. The Soviet Union ultimately abandoned Stalinist economics ... but not until the nation that defeated the techno-economic might of Nazi Germany and launched Sputnik had sunk to the living standards of a less developed country.

The rump of the British car industry finally moved to develop an international, integrated product line ... but as a minor part of Japanese business strategy. The last hold-out against the new electronics in television was Zenith, which held the US market lead in perceived quality. By the time Zenith made the unavoidable switch, its market position had been undermined, condemning the company to a long, losing struggle. Ironically, it was saved only by the electronic

212

revolution: in personal computers, above all in an excellent range of lap-tops, Zenith achieved something of the reputation and penetration irretrievably lost in TVs.

With even greater and sadder irony, in 1989 Zenith was forced to sell its once-profitable computer interests to Groupe Bull of France in order to support its money-eating TV side. In every case where latter-day Luddites have sought to resist, rather than ride the economic, strategic or technological tide (as in all these four examples), the resistance has been futile: far worse, capitulation has only come after years of grievous damage, probably irreversible, and unquestionably a monstrous waste of opportunity and effort.

The curious ability of the Japanese to combine rigid social traditions and respect for the old with insatiable appetite for the new has been a crucial factor in their success. They have deliberately used technological breakpoints to force their way into new markets. With the electric typewriter, the small beginning of office automation, IBM achieved a market leadership as phenomenal as its dominance of mainframes. Slowness to introduce the fully electronic machine – for which IBM should have been singularly well placed – let in the Japanese: they held the ground gained, and IBM has never recovered its losses.

In software (where the producers of the first spreadsheets that launched the PC revolution have disappeared) as in hardware, the information technology industry itself has learnt the imperative of change. To be first may be dangerous, because of the pitfalls of new technology and all start-ups. But it's far more dangerous not to be a quick second – quick to see the potential of innovations, quick to learn the lessons of the pioneers, quick to improve on the innovation, quick to enter the marketplace in force, quick to broaden the market with new products.

In old English, "quick" was the common word for "alive" – as in "the quick and the dead". Those who are not quick to join the office revolution face an increasing risk of commercial death, and not necessarily a lingering one. Yet the transition required is not difficult. Every business is now a customer of the IT industry: every office, no matter how small, has one or more of the new marvels ... a fax machine, perhaps (of which Britain had half a million installed by end-1989, out of no less than 7 million worldwide); or a personal computer for handling the more important pieces of structured work (world PC sales quadrupled to 8 million between 1983 and 1989), or a high-performance copier, a word processor, and so on.

It's a small conceptual step from purchasing and replacing this equipment by ones and twos to filling the gaps and integrating the complete system to undertake both structured and unstructured tasks. Companies have been falling at this first low hurdle, however, because it turns several isolated, minor, relatively cheap tactical decisions into a single, major, apparently expensive strategic choice. That lazy-minded conservatism shuts the door on a vista of endless opportunity.

As the previous chapter argued, management is changing, anyway, moving in precisely the same direction as that demanded by the new technology. To repeat, technology never happens by accident: it is born, or more accurately reborn (for discoveries usually lurk around for decades, waiting for their historical opportunity), in response to need. The rapidly changing markets of today demand flexible management; rapid change and flexibility cannot be achieved in the absence of highly responsive and creative office systems; the two are literally made for each other.

By the mid-nineties, according to consultants Butler Cox, who can claim to have predicted the rise of personal computing before its largely unheralded advent, there will be one PC to every office desk – three times the end-eighties penetration. Before then, the consumption of electric power in offices will have multiplied fourfold. That is the measurable dimension of the revolution. The accompanying development in the management and office culture cannot be measured: but the shock of this quake will rank equally high on the Richter scale of change.

In a period when the technology described by this book will become as ubiquitous as Biro's pen, the shock will be felt most severely by those who have not anticipated and exploited today's developments – even though they can be seen, rather than foreseen. As its opening pages observed, this book has not been an exercise in futurology. The process is happening now, and it won't stop. The modern corporation is sentenced to permanent, perpetual, rapid change. The office revolution is its remedy, its response and its ultimate reprieve.

INDEX

215